Using Mentor Texts to Teach 6 + 1 Writing Traits

In this book, you'll find a wealth of mini lessons designed to improve the quality of students' writing. Each lesson uses a key mentor text and spotlights one of the 6 + 1 Writing Traits to allow students to focus on the essential aspects of good writing – content, organization, word choice, voice, sentence fluency, conventions, and presentation. Inviting and practical, the lessons are concise and follow a consistent model for easy implementation. With seven lessons per chapter, each includes step-by-step guidance, open-ended prompts, and suggestions for additional suitable mentor texts. The chapters are organized by genre – including fiction, informational texts, and poetry – and feature graphic novels and graphic informational mentor texts to inspire and engage students. Aligned with the Common Core State Standards, this resource is essential for any K-8 or pre-service teacher who wants to instill in their students the skills to become independent, confident writers.

Beverly A. DeVries is Professor Emerita at Southern Nazarene University, USA and teaches ESL to elementary students and adults. She is the author of the bestselling textbook *Literacy Assessment and Intervention for Classroom Teachers*, Sixth Edition.

T0386513

Using Mentor Texts to Teach 6 + 1 Writing Traits
Mini Lessons for K-8 Teachers

Beverly A. DeVries

Routledge
Taylor & Francis Group

NEW YORK AND LONDON

Cover image: © Getty Images

First published 2023
by Routledge
605 Third Avenue, New York, NY 10158

and by Routledge
4 Park Square, Milton Park, Abingdon, Oxon, OX14 4RN

Routledge is an imprint of the Taylor & Francis Group, an informa business

© 2023 Taylor & Francis

The right of Beverly A. DeVries to be identified as the author of this work has been asserted in accordance with sections 77 and 78 of the Copyright, Designs and Patents Act 1988.

Trademark notice: Product or corporate names may be trademarks or registered trademarks, and are used only for identification and explanation without intent to infringe.

ISBN: 978-1-032-25491-3 (hbk)
ISBN: 978-1-032-22939-3 (pbk)
ISBN: 978-1-003-28347-8 (ebk)

DOI: 10.4324/9781003283478

Typeset in Palatino
by Apex CoVantage, LLC

This book is dedicated to my husband Merlyn who encourages me and gives me time to do what I love to do—write. Thank you!

Contents

Meet the Author

Beverly A. DeVries has taught writing for over 39 years. Over the years she realized that many teachers emphasized reading skills, but not the art of writing. She firmly believes that examining authors' writing craft aids students in becoming better writers and that they learn to appreciate what authors do to make their texts interesting to read and reread.

DeVries' last 23 years of teaching were in the Education Department at Southern Nazarene University where she stressed to future teachers the importance of teaching writing in a manner that made writing as much fun for students as it was for them to enjoy a good book.

DeVries is now retired but is still very involved in teaching literacy. Her students now are elementary to adult English learners. Presently she is the volunteer director for teaching English as a second language to Afghan refugees and immigrants from Romania, Mexico, Cuba, Venezuela, Columbia, Peru, and Bolivia. She is also involved in reviewing programs for the International Literacy Association.

DeVries received her doctorate in education from Oklahoma State University. Her mentor professor taught her to always seek a new challenge and try something new every day! To Dr. David Yellin, she says, "Thank you!"

Preface

This resource book is intended for undergraduate and graduate education majors and for primary and elementary teachers who are seeking mini lessons to teach the art of writing by analyzing mentor texts. There are six chapters: Primary Fiction, Elementary Fiction, Primary Informational Texts, and Elementary Informational Texts. Primary Poetry, and Elementary Poetry. Each chapter's mini-lesson highlights a mentor text to teach the 6 + 1 Writing Traits: content, organization, word choice, voice, sentence fluency, conventions, and presentation (Northwest Regional Education Laboratory, 2001). The lessons are aligned with the Common Core State Standards (National Governors Association Center for Best Practices (NGACBP) & Council of Chief School Officers (CCSS), 2010).

It was difficult to choose only one mentor text to use for each trait; thus each chapter lists three additional mentor texts that can be used for additional mini-lessons.

I attempted to choose texts that are easy for teachers to locate. Many of the texts may be found in classroom libraries, school libraries, or community libraries. Since many elementary students enjoy the graphic novels and graphic informational texts, I used them as the main mentor text for some lessons.

The mini-lessons provide open-ended questions for teachers to guide students into an understanding of the craft that authors use as they write. It is important that young students consider what makes stories, informational texts, and poetry interesting to read and reread. Mini-lessons are often thought of as an opening to a writing workshop; however, I also view mini lessons to be used during Guided Writing small groups so that teachers can closely observe how each student responds to the open-ended questions and how they improve their writing skills.

The 6 + 1 Writing Traits provides teachers an excellent framework to use when teaching the art of writing to first through twelfth graders. The traits consider the content, organization, word choice, voice, sentence fluency, conventions, and presentation of the pieces. Does the story, informational text, or poem give a unique perspective on the topic? Does the word choice provide readers with a vivid image? Does the author's voice come through the passage? Does the sentence fluency use different types of sentences such as simple sentences with embedded phrases and compound and complex so that the text flows well?

There are seven lessons in each chapter, featuring the 6 + 1 Traits, one main mentor text, and three other suggested additional texts. Each lesson also includes a figure that teachers can use for discussion and/or for students to use as they make notes for their future writing.

Finally, I do not suggest that teachers use the open-ended questions as a script but rather as a guide to carefully study and teach the craft of writing.

1

Primary Fiction

Introduction

The Northwest Regional Education Laboratory studied characteristics of good writing and developed the $6+1$ Trait Writing Model of Instruction & Assessment. Many primary through high school teachers use this model when teaching students the art of writing. The traits have students focus their attention on content, organization, word choice, voice, sentence fluency, conventions, and presentation. The mini-lessons in this text align these traits with a mentor text that models one or more of the traits.

Chapter 1 highlights mini-lessons based on quality children's fiction that are appropriate for primary grades. Each of the seven mini lessons focuses on one of the 6 + 1 Writing Traits and one mentor text with three additional suggested texts. These mini-lessons include open-ended questions that teachers can use to guide students as they examine the craft that authors use when they write engaging stories. The purpose of each mini-lesson is for teachers to guide students as they examine and discover the author's technique rather than teachers telling students what the author did. Each mini-lesson suggests three additional mentor texts that can be used to teach the featured trait.

The first mini-lesson focuses on a book's content. Often primary students have a difficult time choosing a topic for their story; they think it has to be "far-fetched." To get students

DOI: 10.4324/9781003283478-1

started, teachers should help students understand that authors often write about personal experiences. Thus, the first story *Those shoes* (Boelts, 2007) was chosen because students of all ages have ideas of things they want but do not really need; thus it is a topic they can write about because they have knowledge of their needs vs. wants. The three additional mentor texts are about a pet, an imaginary friend, and a traditional folk tale.

The second mini-lesson in this chapter highlights how authors create stories that are well organized. For many students relating an event in chronological order is a challenge. Therefore, I used for the focused mentor text *Can I be your dog?* (Cummings, 2018) that is told through letters written by the dog. This type of organization gives students a fresh idea in which to organize their stories.

Word choice, the third 6 + 1 Writing Trait, is often a focus of writing lessons in the upper grades; however, primary teachers should help students examine the vivid verbs and adjectives that authors choose. Selecting books with vivid words such as *Chrysanthemum* (Henkes, 2008) helps students understand that choosing vivid words results in an engaging story.

There are many fiction books for primary students that have characters with a strong voice. Sometimes the text is written in the first person such as in Daywait's book *The day the crayons quit* (2013). The crayons get very upset with Duncan and they share their emotions in their letters to Duncan. The focused text *Julius: The baby of the world* (Henkes, 1995) displays the protagonist Lily displaying strong emotions about her baby brother Julius's arrival into the family. Her attitude changes throughout the story, which demonstrates to students that their characters' attitudes can change in their stories also.

Sentence fluency, the fifth trait, becomes evident to students when teachers have them focus on the different sentence lengths that authors use. They realize that many short choppy sentences or run-on sentences connected with *ands* do not sound fluent. Having students read their stories aloud and listen to themselves can help students understand that varying sentence length makes their stories sound polished. The featured text "Dear Baby Bear" in *Dear Peter Rabbit* (Flor Ada, 1994) has sentences that vary in length.

With beginning writers, teachers often have students focus on capital letters and ending punctuation. However, the more books teachers share with students, the more they can have students discover that authors use unique marks when characters talk. There are many excellent books that demonstrate the correct usage of quotation marks and punctuation within the quotation marks. Brosgol's *Memory jars* (2021), the focused mentor, has many examples of direct quotations.

Every reader, young and old, enjoys a book with positive eye appeal. Presentation is the + 1 of the 6 + 1 Writing Trait. *The camping trip* (Mann, 2020) is a unique version of a graphic novel. The double-paged illustrations aid students in visualizing the plot's setting as the story progresses. This book because of its unique format draws the reader into the story. This book gives students another idea for presenting their stories.

Grade Level: Primary

Trait: Content

Genre: Fiction

Mentor Text: *Those Shoes*

Author: Maribeth Boelts

Objective: "Write a narrative in which they recount a well-elaborated event or short sequence of events. Include details to describe actions, thought and feeling, use temporal words to signal event order, and provide a sense of closure" (CCSS.ELS-Literacy.W.2.3).

Procedure:

1. Read the book, holding the book so students can view the picture.
2. After reading the book, lead the students in a discussion, asking open-ended questions.
   a. Who is telling the story? How do you know that?
   b. What are the emotions of the narrator as the story progresses?
   c. Does the narrator's mood change? If so, why?
   d. Do the words or the illustrations tell readers more about the character?
   Explain.
3. How is the narrator feeling when he states: "At school, Antonio is smiling big in his brand-new shoes. I feel happy when I look at his face and mad when I look at my Mr. Alfrey shoes" (n. p.).
4. What is the difference between "needs" and "wants"? Record on the board some of their responses.
5. Pass out the "Working Idea" sheet found in Figure 1.1.
6. Give students a couple of minutes to write down some ideas they could write about if they wrote a story about their wants vs. needs

7. Invite students to share some of their ideas.
8. Encourage students to keep this page in their folder so that they have ideas for future writing.
9. Additional mentor text
   a. Brett, J. (1989). *The mitten*. G. P. Putnam's Sons. This mentor text based on a Ukrainian folk tale has an easy plot for primary students to replicate. Teachers can also share Brett's two other books, based on this folk tale: *The hat* (1997) and *The umbrella* (2004)
   b. Jackson, E. (2010). *A home for Dixie: The true story of a rescued puppy*. Turtleback Books. This mentor text about a rescued puppy is a good one to demonstrate to primary students to write about their pets.
   c. Polacco, P. (2005). *Emma Kate*. Philomel Books. This mentor text about an imaginary friend gives students another idea for a topic for a story. As teachers do a read-aloud, they can make sure that students understand that the elephant is an imaginary friend, not a real one.

Genre: Fiction

Mentor Text: *Those Shoes*

Author: Maribeth Boelts

Working Idea Table

Needs vs. Wants	Possible Story Plots

TRAIT: CONTENT
FIGURE 1.1

Grade Level: Primary
Trait: Organization
Genre: Fiction
Mentor Text: *Can I Be Your Dog?*
Author: Troy Cummings
Objective: "Write a narrative in which they recount a well-elaborated event or short sequence of events. Include details to describe actions, thoughts, and feelings, use temporal words to signal event order, and provide a sense of closure" (CCSS.ELA-Literacy.W.2.3).

Procedure:

1. Project the title page and lead the students in an open-ended discussion.
   a. What do you predict the story is about?
   b. Why do they think the dog has a pencil in his mouth?
2. Before reading the first letter, show the first page (letter) and have students predict what the story is about by asking open-ended questions.
   a. Whom do you think is telling the story?
   b. What do you notice about the font?
   c. Does anyone know what the P.S. means?
   d. What do you think the mood of the dog is? Explain.
   e. Whose signature do you think this is?
3. Read the first letter.
   a. Do you think the information that Arfy includes in the letter is important? Explain.
   b. What other information should Arfy include to persuade the people to make him their pet?
4. Read the second letter.
   a. What do you think about Honeywells' tone in the response?
   b. What emotions is Arfy showing in the illustration?

5. Read the rest of the book.
   a. What did you notice about the position of each letter on the page?
   b. Is each letter on the same type of paper? Explain which one is your favorite.
   c. How do the different types of paper reflect the person who wrote the letter? Give examples.
   d. Did the illustrations help tell the story?
   e. How does Arfy's mood change throughout the story?
   f. Did the illustrations help you comprehend the story? Explain.
   g. Ask students to think about the organization of the book and if they think it is well organized or if they think it could be organized differently.
   h. Pair students and give them a few minutes to brainstorm what type of letters they could add to this book. Have them record ideas in Figure 1.2.
   i. Give students an opportunity to share ideas.
6. Additional Mentor Texts
   a. Brett, J. (2004). *The umbrella*. G. P. Putman's Sons. This story builds from one creature after the other jumping unto the umbrella. Students can think of another object other than the umbrella, hat, or mitten to create a new story.
   b. Numeroff, L. J. (1985). *If you give a mouse a cookie*. HarperCollins. This text is organized as cause/effect. Discuss the cause and the effects and how this progression creates the plot. This with Numeroff's other *If you . . .* books are organized as cause/effect, which may challenge students to write a similar story.
   c. Willems, M. (2004). *The pigeon finds a hot dog!* Hyperion Books for Children. This mentor text is organized around a dialogue between two characters. Students can be encouraged to think of two characters such as a cat and a dog and imagine the two creatures arguing over the same space or the same toy.

Trait: Organization

Mentor Text: *Can I Be Your Dog?*

Author: Troy Cummings

Name to Whom the Letter is Addressed	Main Idea of What Information Is in the Letter

GENRE: FICTION
FIGURE 1.2

Grade Level: Primary

Trait: Word Choice

Genre: Fiction

Mentor Text: *Chrysanthemum*

Author: Kevin Henkes

Objective: "Use sentence-level context as a clue to the meaning of words or phrases" (CCSS.ELA-Literacy.L.2.4.a).

Procedure:

1. Do a read-aloud with the text, emphasizing Chrysanthemum's shifting emotions throughout the story.
2. Go back and read through the pages when she arrives home after her first day of school, emphasizing *dreadful* and *miserable*. Ask open-ended questions.
   a. What do you think *dreadful* means? Using Figure 1.3, record their responses and circle the one(s) that is closest to the meaning.
   b. What do you think *miserable* means? Again record their responses.
3. Read the line, in which her father states: "And precious and priceless and fascinating and winsome."
   a. What does *precious* mean? Record their responses and circle the word that is closest to the meaning.
   b. What does *priceless* mean?
   c. What does *fascinating* mean?
   d. What does *winsome* mean?
   e. Do you think these are good word choices? Why?

4. Next turn to the page when Chrysanthemum comes home the second day and ask students the meaning of the following words, leading them in an open-ended discussion.
   a. Envious, begrudging, discontented, jaundiced.
   b. Are these good word choices? Explain.
5. Is Chrysanthemum totally content when it says she "felt a trifle better after her favorite dessert"?
   a. What does *trifle* mean?
6. Reread the page on the second night and the dream she had.
   a. What are the meanings of *sprouted*, *plucked*, and *scrawny*?
7. Reread the page after Mrs. Twinkly announced that she was considering Chrysanthemum as her baby's named and discussed the words *blushed, beamed,* and *bloomed.*
   a. What is the initial letter of these three words? What is that called?
   b. What do these words tell you about Chrysanthemum?
8. Hang Figure 1.3 in the Writing Center so students can refer to it when they are writing. Remind students to use descriptive words when they write.
9. Additional Mentor Texts
   a. Alexander, L. (2000). *How the cat swallowed thunder.* Puffin Books. This mentor text has rich word choice throughout the story. Students can determine their meanings by the context of the sentences. Some words include: *topsy-turvy, leaky, amiss, fetched, eiderdown quilt, flung, spattered, nasty, goose-feather blizzard*, and many more!
   b. Henkes, K. (1996). *Lilly's purple plastic purse.* Green-willow. The title of this mentor text demonstrates to students how they can use alliteration in stories. The page in which Mr. Slinger is returning Lily's purse has a phrase that has rhythm: "students were

buttoned and zipped and snapped and tied." On that page and a few pages after that there are descriptive words: *jingly, fabulous, disturbed, lurched*.

c. Wood, A. (2000). *Jubal's wish*. The Blue Sky Press. This mentor text has excellent word choice throughout the book, including some onomatopoeia: *whackity-whack, grumped, heaved, stomped, plopped*, and *bobbed*.

Genre: Fiction

Mentor Text: *Chrysanthemum*

Author: Kevin Henkes

Word	Meaning
Dreadful	
Miserable	
Precious	
Priceless	
Fascinating	
Envious	

TRAIT: WORD CHOICE
FIGURE 1.3

Grade Level: Primary
Trait: Voice
Genre: Fiction
Mentor Text: *Julius: The Baby of the World*
Author: Kevin Henkes
Objective: "Use dialogue and descriptions of actions, thoughts, and feelings to develop experiences and events or show the response of characters to situations" (CCSS. ELA-Literacy.W.3.3.b).

Procedure:

1. Read the book and fill in the story map (Figure 1.4) as you stop to discuss the following.
   a. How did Lilly feel before Julius was born?
      i. What details of the story indicate that feeling?
   b. How did Lilly feel after Julius was born?
      i. What actions of Lilly indicate that feeling?
      ii. What were Lilly's feelings about his nose? Eyes? Fur?
      iii. What did Lilly say about Julius when her parents were admiring him?
      iv. What did Lilly do when they told her to tell him stories?
      v. When she sang him numbers and letters?
      vi. When she told him a story about the Germ?
      vii. What do these actions tell readers about Lilly's feelings?
   c. Discuss how her attitude changes during the following exchange. Reread with expression beginning with "'Disgusting,' said Cousin Garland. 'What?' said Lilly." And ending with "'Now repeat after me . . . Julius is the baby of the world . . . Louder!'"

d. Explain that when authors write the way Henkes wrote, the author is giving voice to the characters. Authors use dialogue and action to relate to readers all the feelings of the protagonist.

2. Additional Mentor Texts

   a. Daywait, D. (2013). *The day the crayons quit*. Philomel. Each crayon is upset with Duncan for either using that crayon too much or not using the crayon enough. The letters written by each crayon express strong emotions. The teacher can use only one example to demonstrate how Daywait used voice to create a hilarious story.

   b. Stevens, J., & Stevens Crummel, S. (1999). *Cook-a-doodle-doo!* Harcourt Brace & Company. It is clear to readers that Big Brown Rooster is not happy with his feed and wants something new. However, it appears that no one is listening; thus there is no hope. As he gathers his animal friends to help, there is a disaster! Big Brown Rooster gets extremely bossy as his friends do not understand the meaning of words as they relate to baking (e.g. beat an egg, cut butter, cut a measuring cup to make 3/4 cup).

   c. Willems, M. (2004). *The pigeon finds a hot dog!* Hyperion. Pigeon becomes very bossy and impatient with Duckling when Pigeon has a hot dog and it is clear to the reader that Duckling is attempting to get it from Pigeon. Willems uses larger and darker print as Pigeon becomes more frustrated with Duckling. Reading this aloud, teachers can make it very clear that Pigeon has a strong voice!

Mentor Text: *Julius: The Baby of the World*

Author: Kevin Henkes

Add Lily's actions/emotions at each part of the story.

Lily Before Julius' Birth

Lily After Julius' Birth

Garland's Reaction to Julius
Lily's Reaction to Garland

GENRE: FICTION
FIGURE 1.4

Grade Level: Primary

Trait: Sentence Fluency

Genre: Fiction

Mentor Text: *Dear Peter Rabbit*

Author: Alma Flor Ada

Objective: "Produce, expand, and rearrange complete simple and compound sentences" (CCSS ELA-Literacy.L.2.2).

Dear Peter Rabbit can also be found at the following site. Copy and paste the web address in the URL bar.

www.youtube.com/watch?v=XycinqhIAY8

You can fast forward the book to Goldilocks' letter.

Procedure

1. Share the background of the book *Dear Peter Rabbit* so students understand that each page is a different letter from one fairy tale character to another.
2. Read the first letter from Goldilocks, or listen to the letter on the site given.
3. Using Figure 1.5, project the third paragraph from the first letter written by Goldilocks found in "Dear Baby Bear" so all students can read it. Lead them in open-ended questions.
   a. What did the author do to separate the names of the different vegetables? Did that make it easy to read and understand?
   b. Discuss how the author lets readers know when the action takes place with the phrase "Every other night, or so" at the beginning of the sentence. The phrase is followed by a comma.
4. After discussing the first sentence, project the second sentence.

    a. What type of sentence is the first one?

    b. Is it long or short?

    c. What type of sentence is the second sentence?

    d. Is it longer or shorter than the first one?

    e. Explain how the use of shorter and longer sentences creates sentence fluency.

    f. Discuss how the author used only the word *and* to connect two items.

5. After the discussion about the text, project the sentences titled "Example." Invite students to write one sentence, using all the ideas.

6. After a few minutes, ask students to read their sentences to the class.

7. Additional Mentor Text

    a. Numeroff, L., & Evans, N. (2008). *The jellybeans and the big dance*. Scholastic. This mentor text has multiple examples of compound sentences followed by simple and complex sentences. The story begins with a one simple sentence on page 1. Page 2 is a compound-complex sentence. Teachers should read it so students can hear sentence fluency.

    b. Rey, M., & Rey, H. A. (2004). *A treasury of Curious George*. Houghton Mifflin Company. This mentor text has many of the Curious George stories. Pages 86–89 have examples of simple, compound, and complex sentences.

    c. Wood, A. (1984). *The napping house*. Harcourt Brace Jovanovich, Publishers. Many students have heard this book read since they were young children. The primary grades is a good time to show students how Wood used commas to create the cumulative text.

Genre: Fiction

Mentor Text: *Dear Peter Rabbit*

Author: Alma Flor Ada

"Every other night or so, a cabbage, a lettuce, or a carrot is missing" (Flor Ada, 1994, 3rd letter, 3rd paragraph).

"And guess what? Yesterday, after he chased a rabbit out of the garden, my father found a tiny jacket by the fence, and the tiniest pair of shoes between some rows of carrots" (Flor Ada, 1994, 3rd letter, 4th paragraph).

EXAMPLE: Write a sentence or two to show sentence fluency.

Mary likes the pizza.
Mary likes ice cream.
Mary likes peanut butter.
Mary likes hamburgers.
Mary does not like hot dogs.

TRAIT: SENTENCE FLUENCY
FIGURE 1.5

Grade Level: Primary	
Trait: Conventions	
Genre: Fiction	
Mentor Text: *Memory Jars*	
Author: Vera Brosgol	

Objective: "Use knowledge of language and its conventions when writing, speaking, reading, or listening" (CCSS.ELA-Literacy.L2.3).

Procedure:

1. After reading and enjoying the story *Memory jars*, go back to the fourth page (unpaged) of the story and project the text so all students can see.
2. Draw attention to the quotation marks found around Gran's and Freda's dialogue. Lead students in open-ended questions.
    a. Could you "hear" the voices of Gran and Freda? Who wants to read so the class can hear them talk?
    b. Did the dialogue make the story more realistic?
    c. What marks are around what Gran and Freda said? Explain how the words that each character speaks are in quotation marks, but the explanatory words (text that tells readers who is speaking) are not in quotation marks.
    d. What does the author do each time there is a new speaker?
    e. Discuss how the explanatory words for Gran are at the end of the first sentence she speaks but not in the other three sentences. Explain to students how varying the way authors write dialogue creates fluent writing.

    f. Are there quotation marks at the end of this paragraph?

    g. Do you know why there are not any?

    h. Is Gran still talking in this next paragraph?

    i. That is why at the end of the first paragraph there are no quotation marks because Gran keeps speaking in the following paragraph.

3. Turn to page 6 (unpaged) of the story in which Gran and Freda are remembering Grandpa.

    a. What do you think Gran might be saying to Freda?

    b. What is Freda answering in return?

    c. Project and complete Figure 1.6 as a class.

4. Additional Mentor Texts

    a. Erickson, J. R. (1983). *The original adventures of Hank the cowdog*. Meverick Books. Page 88 of this mentor text has good examples of beginning a new paragraph with each new speaker. Using dialogue between speakers creates an interesting story.

    b. Henkes, K. (1996). *Lily's purple plastic purse*. Greenwillow. This mentor text has many examples to use for teaching quotation marks.

    c. Willems, M. (2004). *The pigeon finds a hot dog*. Hyperion Books. This mentor text has multiple examples of when to use question marks, exclamation marks, commas, and periods. The print is large so students can easily see the punctuation when teachers read the text.

Genre: Fiction

Mentor Text: *Memory Jars*

Author: Vera Brosgol

Introducing quotation marks to help stories more interesting.

Discussion should emphasize the following:

*Discuss the question mark BEFORE the quotation mark in the first paragraph.

*Discuss the comma BEFORE the quotation mark in the second paragraph.

*Explain why there is no quotation mark at the end of the second paragraph.

*Discuss why there are quotation marks at the beginning and end of the third paragraph.

Complete this example of what Gran may be asking Freda and what Freda answers in return:

Gran asked Freda, _____?

Freda replied, _____.

TRAIT: CONVENTIONS
FIGURE 1.6

Grade Level: Primary

Trait: Presentation

Genre: Fiction

Mentor Text: *The Camping Trip*

Author: Jennifer K. Mann

Objective: "Write narratives in which they recount a well-elaborated event or short sequence of events, include details to describe actions, thoughts, and feelings; use temporal words to signal event order, and provide a sense of closure" (CCSS.ELA-Literacy.W.2.3).

This mentor text is a graphic novel that primary students can easily comprehend as they read the panels. It is a good one to encourage reluctant writers who are strong artists but who do not care to write. Graphics are simple to draw and the plot is easy to follow. The map to the campsite gives students a unique way to show the change in setting as the story progresses.

Procedure:

1. Read the first page and lead students in open-ended questions.
   a. Who is telling the story?
   b. How can you tell?
2. Read and share pages 1–8 and lead students in a discussion about the presentation of the story.
   a. On pages 1 and 2, what tells the story, the text or illustrations or both?
   b. On pages 3–4, why do you think the author/illustrator used three small panels and one single illustration to show what she packed?

    c. How effective on pages 5 and 6 was it for the author to use panels with text and dialogue bubbles? How did that help tell the story? Could it be done a different way?

    d. On pages 7 and 8 why did the author draw a double-page illustration of the car traveling on a road from the city to the woods with little panels explaining what the narrator and her cousin do in the car? Is that more effective than just text with dialogue? Explain.

3. Which page did you like most? Why?
4. Was it easy to follow the storyline?
5. Invite students to share a morning in which they had to pack a backpack or bag as they got ready for school.
6. Pass out Figure 1.7 and ask students to write/illustrate how they pack their backpacks for school each morning.
7. Additional Mentor Texts

    a. Cummings, T. (2018). *Can I be your dog?* Dragonfly Books. This mentor text is a series of letters written by a dog that is looking for a home. Each letter builds the plot to the climax. Each letter is signed with a dog paw.

    b. Daywait, D. (2013). *The day the crayons quit.* Philomel. This book is a series of letters written by crayons to their user Duncan. Each crayon is upset about the treatment they receive from Duncan.

    c. Fleming, D. (1998). *In the small, small pond.* Henry Holt. This mentor text places words in a variety of ways that express the meaning of the sound of the word.

Genre: Fiction

Mentor Text: *The Camping Trip*

Author/Illustrator: Jennifer K. Mann

Using panels and pencil drawings, illustrate three main things that you do each morning as you get ready for school. Then on the right-hand side of the panels, draw the objects that you pack into your backpack.

TRAIT: PRESENTATION
FIGURE 1.7

2
Elementary Fiction

Introduction

Chapter 2 highlights mini-lessons based on quality fiction that is appropriate for intermediate elementary grades. Each of the seven mini lessons focuses on one of the 6 + 1 Writing Traits. These mini-lessons include open-ended questions that teachers can use to guide students as they examine the craft that authors use when they write engaging picture books and novels. The purpose of each mini-lesson is for teachers to lead students as they examine and discover the author's technique rather than teachers telling students what authors did.

Stories written for elementary students are more sophisticated than for primary students; thus it is important that teachers select picture books and chapter books during mini lessons that align with students' ability as they examine the author's craft. In many of these lessons, I suggest that during shared reading time teachers read the picture book the day before they teach the mini-lesson. If they choose a chapter book, they should focus on only a short passage as demonstrated in these mini-lessons.

The first mini-lesson focuses on a book's content. Chad's *Leo Geo and the cosmic crisis* (2013) is a unique graphic novel; the topic will appeal to elementary students that like plots with many twists. Halfway through the book, readers need to flip to the back of the book to complete the story. As in any graphic novel, the illustrations are as important as the text; therefore, students need

DOI: 10.4324/9781003283478-2

time to view and study the illustrations. Other stories that may appeal to elementary students are the three additional texts. The first is a graphic novel that has panels and additional drawings completed by the protagonist. The second is a story about the boy who did not want to attend a boring family reunion with relatives he did not know, a typical scenario for many elementary students. The third one is a fantasy with well-developed characters and a setting that does not exist, but the author makes it appear to be plausible.

Jangles: A big fish story (Shannon, 2012) begins with a father relating a fishing experience; thus, the plot includes a flashback, which is a good way to organize a story. The open-ended questions in the mini-lesson will help teachers guide students in organizing a story based on a flashback. Barrett's popular *Cloudy with a chance of meatballs* (1982) also includes a similar flashback, as does Salley's *Why Epossumondas has no hair on his tail* (2004). The third additional text has a cause/effect plot, another way to organize a story.

Many teachers focus on vivid word choice. It was difficult to choose only one book to use as the mentor text. I choose *Magnificent homespun brown* (Doyon, 2020) because of its vivid language to describe *brown*. Rosenstock's *Mornings with Monet* (2021), another suggested text, also has vivid verbs. If teachers read the opening passage of Monet getting up in the morning and invite students to pantomime the action, they would do it as the illustration shows Monet did it. A very different text with vivid language is Reynolds' *Pirates and cowboys* (2014). It uses the slang of pirates and cowboys to show the conflict between the two groups. Some young writers may enjoy using slang/dialect in their stories.

The fourth trait, voice, is often omitted when teaching writing skills; however, a strong voice of a protagonist can make a passage of fiction appear to be real. *Encounter* (Yolen, 1992) is a picture book in which the protagonist gives such a strong plea to his elders that readers feel empathy for this young Native American. The last page is a powerful mentor passage to demonstrate how to conclude a story in which the protagonist had a strong voice as heard through his speech and shown in his actions.

Many novels demonstrate sentence fluency, the fifth trait. Creech in her 1994 Newbery Award *Walk two moons* has ample examples of sentence fluency. Reading short passages of this text demonstrates to students how authors vary the sentence length to make the text fluent.

The passage chosen for the sixth mini-lesson of Chapter 2 is filled with grammar and punctuation errors; it was chosen with a purpose. Many students love pointing out errors of other writers. In this mini-lesson students are asked to find the errors, to correct them, and then to analyze if Curtis in *Bud, not Buddy* (1999), another Newbery Award winner, makes the errors to show vivid characterization. They will soon determine that the errors represent the protagonist's voice. The three additional texts demonstrate how to use dashes and ellipses, more sophisticated punctuation marks, correctly.

The mini-lesson for presentation, the + 1 Trait, is a graphic novel with the protagonist's illustrations inserted into this novel to demonstrate how authors give voice to characters through the use of graphics. After the mini-lesson, students who are reluctant writers may be inspired to illustrate a story, using limited text with detailed illustrations to indicate the mood and attitude of the protagonist. Two of the additional novels are *Stepping stones* (Knisley, 2020) and *Dog Man unleashed* (Pilkey, 2017), also graphic novels. Pilkey's novel has many panels without any text; the facial expressions of the characters reveal the attitude of the characters. The third additional text is Richardson and Richardson's *Family reunion* (2021) that demonstrates how differently sized font and unique placement of words can result in a text with great eye appeal.

Grade Level: Elementary

Trait: Content

Genre: Fiction

Mentor Text: *Leo Geo and the Cosmic Crisis*

Author: Jon Chad

Objective: "Use concrete words and sensory details to convey experiences and events precisely" (CCSS.ELA-Literacy.W.5.3.d).

Procedure:

1. Display the first double page and ask students what they observe. Lead students in an open-ended discussion, using the following questions.
   a. What do you think is the main topic of the story?
   b. What illustrations helped you make that decision?
   c. Looking at the details of the illustrations, what do you think the mood of the story is? Why do you think that?
   d. Are all the characters human?
2. Before you begin to read the first five dialogue bubbles, ask students to look closely at the bubbles to determine in which order they should be read.
   a. What did Chad do to help readers in correctly following the bubbles?
   b. What did you notice about the outline of the bubbles? Are they all the same? If not, what do you think the different kinds represent?
3. Turn the page and display the book so students can view the rocket blasting off.
   a. What type of bubbles does Chad use on this page?
   b. Some of the bubbles give readers information about the fuel used in space shuttles and rockets. Is this information accurate?

     c. Is it a good idea for the author to include information in a graphic novel? Explain.

4. Turn to the middle of the book and lead students in more open-ended questions.

     a. What is happening on these pages?

     b. Was it necessary that the author instruct readers to "Flip the book over and start reading from the other end of the book to find out what happened to Leo Geo"?

     c. Is this an effective technique or a confusing technique? Explain.

5. After sharing the entire book, place it in the Reading Center so students can refer back to the book.

6. Invite students to create a graphic novel that uses this type of graphics instead of the usual panels with gutters.

Grade Level: Elementary
Trait: Organization
Genre: Fiction
Mentor Text: *Jangles: A Big Fish Story*
Author: David Shannon
Objective: "Establish a situation and introduce a narrator and/or characters; organize an event sequence that unfolds naturally" (CCSS.ELA-Literacy.W.3.3.a).

Procedure:

1. Read the entire book.
2. After re-reading the first page, project it if possible, and lead students in open-ended questions that will help them understand that Shannon used a flashback to tell the story.
    a. Why do you think Shannon shares that first sentence?
    b. What is the setting for the story?
    c. How does the setting make you feel?
    d. Is there tension in the narrator's voice? If not tension, what feeling does the narrator evoke in readers?
    e. How do you visualize the tackle box? Explain.
    f. How do the details of the tackle box add to the story's mood?
    g. What phrase or sentence lets readers know that this story is a flashback?
3. Project the second paragraph from page one (See Figure 2.1) and read it again.
4. Take note of the punctuation Shannon used at the end of the paragraph of the first page. Explain to students that this is one way authors introduce flashbacks.
5. Re-read the last two pages to show students how Shannon ended the flashback and the story.

    a. What punctuation did Shannon use on the second to last page?

    b. What does the ellipse tell readers?

    c. What does Shannon imply by the information shared in the second to last paragraph of the story?

6. Hand out the Idea page found in Figure 2.2 and pair students. Ask them to generate ideas for stories that they could write, using a flashback.

7. Additional Mentor Texts with Flashbacks.

    a. Barrett, J. (1982). *Cloudy with a chance of meatballs*. Athenaeum Books for Young Readers. Grandpa is flipping pancakes one morning when he begins to tell the grandchildren a tall tale about the town of Chewandswallow that received its food each day from the clouds.

    b. Salley, C. (2004). *Why Epossumondas has no hair on his tail*. Harcourt, Inc. Epossumondas is wondering why he does not have a bushy tail like skunks, foxes, and hares. Mama began to tell him about Papapossum, his great-great-grandpa who did have a fluffy tail until Bear got his tail and pulled and pulled it until it was long with no hair.

    c. Willems, M. (2019). *Because*. Hyperion Books for Children. This mentor text demonstrates how an author creates a cause/effect plot. Each page begins with *because* and simply tells of an event, which caused another event to happen. It begins with Beethoven composing beautiful music that caused Franz to write his own music that caused an orchestra to form. Later someone had a cold, which caused a little girl to have the opportunity to go hear beautiful music that inspired her to eventually take center stage. The text is terse so readers can readily follow the cause/effect plot.

Trait: Organization

Genre: Fiction

Mentor Text: *Jangles: A Big Fish Story*

Author: David Shannon

With a classmate, brainstorm ideas for a possible story that has a flashback. Think of as many ideas as possible.

The Main Plot of Story	Opening/Setting of Story That Leads to the Flashback

FIGURE 2.1

Grade Level: Elementary

Trait: Word Choice

Genre: Fiction

Mentor Text: *Magnificent Homespun Brown*

Author: Samara Cole Doyon

Objective: "Use concrete words and phrases and sensory details to convey experiences and events precisely" (CCSS. ELA-Literacy.W.4.3.d).

Procedure:

1. Read the entire book at a pace that fits the mood.
2. Pass out Figure 2.3 so students can record the words and phrases you discuss.
3. Lead the students in a discussion with open-ended questions.
   a. What color is *deep, secret brown?* What other words could you use for the same color?
   b. What are *subtly churning river currents?* Can someone pantomime how the currents would be moving?
   c. How does something "playfully beckon" a person?
   d. When the text states *through my grandmother's kitchen window*, where is the narrator standing? Inside or outside? Explain.
   e. What do readers see on the riverbanks?
   f. What does the following mean: "carrying miles of life and endless possibility"?
   g. Is the story full of conflict? Explain.
   h. How does the sentence flow create a mood for readers?
   i. What other word choices painted vivid pictures in your mind? Record them in the Table of Figure 2.3.
4. Additional Mentor Texts

a. Mafi, T. (2016). *Furthermore*. Dutton Children's Books. This mentor text has many examples of vivid word choices that permit readers to visualize the scene. For example: "Wind unlocking windows; rain light nudging curtains apart; fresh-cut grass tickling unsocked feet" (Mafi, 2016, p. 4).

b. Reynolds, A. (2014). *Pirates vs. cowboys*. Alfred A. Knopf. This mentor text demonstrates how to use dialect by two opposing groups. The excellent word choice found in the dialect makes the plot humorous.

c. Rosenstock, B. (2021). *Mornings with Monet*. Alfred A. Knope. This mentor text demonstrates vivid verb usage that makes it possible for readers to visualize the action.

Mentor Text: *Magnificent Homespun Brown*

Author: Samara Cole Doyon

Record the phrases discussed in class and any other words you and your classmates thought created vivid pictures in readers' minds.

Words or Phrase	Meaning
deep, secret brown	
subtly churning	
miles of life	
endless possibilities	

GENRE: FICTION
FIGURE 2.2

Grade Level: Elementary

Trait: Voice

Genre: Fiction

Mentor Text: *Encounter*

Author: Jane Yolen

Objective: "Provide a conclusion that follows from the narrated experiences or events" (CCSS.ELA-Literacy.W.5.3.e).

Note: The narrator has a strong voice throughout the story, and the last page is a great passage to teach students how to write a strong conclusion with a strong voice so readers can contemplate the injustice shared in the story.

If you do not have it, it is a great one to add to your classroom library.

Procedure:

1. Read and discuss the text during shared reading time on a day previous to the one in which you use this text for reviewing voice and focusing on writing strong conclusions.
2. Project Figure 2.4 so all students can see it. Be sure all students have a paper copy so they can add the notes as you write them on the whiteboard.
3. Lead students in open-ended questions.
    a. What are some words the author used to show the narrator's strong feelings about these strangers?
    b. Is the verb *begged* a better word choice than *asked*? Explain.
    c. How does the word *spat* help readers visualize the narrator's attitude? Is there a better word that could be used?

    d. What does the author mean by the phrase *men but not men*?

    e. How do you think the narrator felt when the strangers patted him on his head? Explain.

    f. Explain what the narrator is conveying when he states that "We took their speech into our mouths, forgetting our own" (Yolen, last page).

    g. Explain how their sons and daughters became the strangers' sons and daughters. How does that make the narrator feel? Explain.

    h. What feelings are evoked when you read that he, an old man, has no more dreams?

4. Additional Mentor Texts

    a. Craft, J. (2019). *New kid*. Harper/Harper Collins Publishers. In this graphic novel, Craft used pencil drawings of the narrator to display his strong dislike for his new school and the kids in the school. The illustrations with the terse text give a powerful voice to Jordan, the narrator.

    b. Reynolds, P. H. (2003). *The dot*. Candlewick Press. The main character of this mentor text has strong feelings about her inability to paint.

    c. Richardson, C., & Richardson, D. (2021). *Family reunion*. Barefoot Books. The young boy voices his objection to attending a family reunion of relatives he does not know. He wants to stay home and play video games. His parents demand he attends; which he does do. His attitude toward his relatives changes as he hears them voicing loving affection for one another.

Genre: Fiction

Mentor Text: *Encounter*

Author: Jane Yolen

Pass out a copy of this table so students can take notes during class discussion. The bold words were added for emphasis.

Page #	Quote	Comments About Voice
2	"I begged."	
3	"canoes spat"	
3	"men but not men."	
12	"We were patted on the head"	
17	"We took their speech into our mouths, forgetting our own."	
17	"Our sons and daughters became *their* sons and daughters."	
17	"I, an old man now, dream no more dreams."	

TRAIT: VOICE
FIGURE 2.3

Grade Level: Elementary

Trait: Sentence Fluency

Genre: Fiction

Mentor Text: *Walk Two Moons*

Author: Sharon Creech

Objective: "Use knowledge of language and its conventions when writing, speaking, reading, or listening" (CCSS. ELA-Literacy.L.5.3).

Because Creech's works depict sentence fluency, the novel also is good mentor text to demonstrate advanced conventions such as hyphenated words and colons to set off a series.

1. *Walk two moons* is a great book to use for a Book Talk to generate students' interest in reading it. The plot has many twists and the book reflects Creech's ability to display sentence fluency.
2. After a Book Talk, project the quote found in Figure 2.5 so all students can see it.
3. Ask students open-ended questions.
   a. What type of sentence (e.g. simple, compound, complex, compound-complex) is the first sentence?
   b. What type of sentence is the last sentence?
   c. Would it be better if Creech had used two long sentences? Explain.
   d. Would it be better if Creech used many short sentences to list the objects the narrator took from her mother's closet?
   e. What convention did Creech use before she lists the three things?
   f. Does the colon aid readers in comprehending that Creech is "announcing" the items that she took?

    g. What punctuation does Creech use to separate the items in the series? Why did she use them?

    h. How does Creech describe the dress?

    i. Why do you think she calls it a *yellow-flowered cotton dress* instead of saying it was a cotton dress with yellow flowers? How different would the sentence read, if she did say it was a cotton dress with yellow flowers?

    j. What did Creech use between *yellow* and *flowered*?

4. Explain that authors often use hyphenated adjectives to create sentence fluency.

5. Ask students to look at their clothes and think of a hyphenated adjective to describe their clothes.

6. Give students a few minutes to practice using a colon and hyphenated adjectives by projecting Figure 2.6.

Genre: Fiction

Mentor Text: *Walk Two Moons*

Author: Sharon Creech

In my bureau were three things of hers that I had taken from her closet after she left: a red, fringed shawl; a blue sweater; and a yellow-flowered cotton dress that was always my favorite. These things had her smell on them.

(p. 196)

From the following information write a sentence, using a colon and hyphenated adjectives to create a passage with sentence fluency.

Joe will only wear

Shoes that are red and white

Shoes with checks

Shoes with blue laces

Jeans that are flared

Jeans that are dark blue

Shirt that is white

Shirt that has red stripes

Shirt that has long sleeves

TRAIT: SENTENCE FLUENCY
FIGURE 2.4

Grade Level: Elementary

Trait: Conventions

Genre: Fiction (Chapter book)

Mentor Text: *Bud, Not Buddy*

Author: Christopher Paul Curtis

Objective: "Demonstrate command of the conventions of standard English capitalization, punctuation, and spelling when writing" (CCSS.ELA-Literacy. L.5.2).

Note to teachers: This passage has many punctuation and capitalization errors. I chose the passage to see if students recognized them and to get them to discuss if the errors created a mood for the story.

Procedure:

1. Project the short passage from the text as found in Figure 2.6.
2. Read the passage as it is found on page 133.
3. Using open-ended questions, lead students in a discussion about the conventions.
   a. Are there any grammar errors? If so, where? Would you change the grammar? If so, why? If not, why not?
   b. Are there any punctuation errors? If so, where? Would you change them? If so, why? If not, why not?
   c. Are there any capitalization errors? If so, why do you think Curtis used them?
   d. Do you think any of these conventions should be changed? Why or why not?
   e. Do the errors make the writing more authentic? Explain.
4. Pair the students and using the beginning line in Figure 2.6, ask them to write a short passage, adding to that line. Share their writings with classmates.

a. Floca, B. (2009). *Moonshot*. Athenaeum Books for young Readers. This text has multiple examples of the proper use of ellipses and dashes.

b. Peck, R. (2000). *A year down yonder*. Dial Books. Throughout the book, Peck demonstrates how to use quotation marks correctly and to begin a new paragraph with each new speaker. For example, page 99 has dialogue back and forth between Grandma and the stranger who was painting a mural.

c. Willems, M. (2019). *In Because*. Willems demonstrates proper use of the dash in this text.

Genre: Fiction (Chapter book)

Mentor Text: *Bud, Not Buddy*

Author: Christopher Paul Curtis

"RULES AND THINGS NUMBER 8

Whenever an Adult Tells You to Listen
Carefully and Talks to You in a Real Calm Voice Do
Not Listen, Run as Fast as You can Because
Something Real Terrible Is Just Around the
Corner. Especially If the Cops Are Chasing You."
(Curtis, 1999, p. 133.)

Invite students to complete the following line. Tell them they may use any type of convention error.

Whenever your parent tells you to. . . .

TRAIT: CONVENTIONS
FIGURE 2.5

Grade Level: Elementary

Trait: Presentation

Genre: Graphic Novel

Mentor Text: *New Kid*

Author/Illustrator: Jerry Craft (2019). Harper/HarperCollins Publishers.

Objective: "Use narrative techniques, such as dialogue, description, and pacing, to develop experiences and events or show the responses of characters to situations" (CCSS.ELA-Literacy.W.5.3.b).

Note: Teachers should remind students that since the narrative in graphic novels is terse, authors use detailed illustrations to relate the characters' attitudes and personalities. Craft, the author of *New kid*, also used pencil drawings by the main character Jordan to depict Jordan's personality and attitude toward his new school.

Procedure:

1. Briefly share the pages listed in #2 with students to indicate that Craft inserts pencil drawings, created by the protagonist, to show how he feels about specific actions.
2. After briefly sharing the pages, **select one** of the protagonist's drawings and go into greater detail on how the author exposes Jordan's personality through his drawings.
   a. Pages 4–6 – black and white pencil drawings of the main character Jordan's "Back To School Drawing."
      i. What do readers learn about Jordan in this drawing?
      ii. Do readers think that Jordan likes school?
      iii. Who is running away from the books, ruler, and calculator?

    b. Pages 8–9 – Jordan's drawing of "My Dad's Tips For Being a Man! 'Shaking Hands' "
        i. Ask students if they think the illustrations are a good representation of the terse label of the handshakes. Give reasons for their stance.
        ii. Discuss what is meant by "And the most important rule of all: never, ever give someone a "dead fish!!!"
    c. Pages 40–41 – The DUDE Pyramid: A Guide to Cafeteria Heirarchy:
        i. Did Jordan misspell *hierarchy* with a purpose? If so, what was the purpose?
        ii. What group of students does the fox depict? The squirrels? The lions? The mice? The worms?
        iii. What do the drawings tell readers about Jordan and his relationship to other students at the school?
    d. Pages 56–57 – Jordan's Tips for Taking the Bus
        i. Jordan explains in this drawing that fitting in on the ride to school is hard work. Why does he say that?
        ii. Do your students change their ways when they are around different types of kids? Have them explain.
        iii. What type of illustration would your students draw to depict their experience with different groups?

3. Discuss the effectiveness or ineffectiveness of the author's technique of developing character through drawings by the protagonist.

4. Pass out the sheet in Figure 2.7 and give students a few minutes to illustrate their Back-To-School Feelings.

5. **Additional Mentor Texts**
    a. Knisley, L. (2020). *Stepping stones*. A graphic novel in which the author used the protagonist's drawings to depict her attitude about her becoming a blended family.

b. Pilkey, D. (2017). *Dog Man unleashed*. Graphix/ Scholastic. This graphic novel has many panels without any text. This type of graphic novel might appeal to students who are good artists. The facial expressions of the characters reveal much of the attitudes of the characters.

c. Richardson, C., & Richardson, D. (2021). *Family reunion*. The presentation is eye-catching with all the different size fonts and placements. There are brown/ white drawings within the illustrations. Both of these features give eye appeal that students can use in their writing.

Genre: Graphic Novel

Mentor Text: *New Kid*

Author/Illustrator: Jerry Craft (2019).

Invite students to illustrate four panels depicting their attitude about being a new kid in a school; or if they have never changed schools, depict their attitude about starting a new school year.

TRAIT: PRESENTATION
FIGURE 2.6

3

Informational Primary Texts

Introduction

Chapter 3 highlights seven mini-lessons based on quality children's informational texts that are appropriate for primary grades. Like the first two chapters, each of the seven mini lessons focuses on one of the 6 + 1 Writing Traits. The highlighted texts in this chapter have photographs instead of illustrations. These mini-lessons include open-ended questions that guide students to examine the craft that authors use when they write engaging informational texts. The purpose of each mini-lesson is for teachers to guide students as they examine and discover the author's technique; teachers should not merely "tell" students what authors did.

The first mini-lesson focuses on gathering content that is appropriate for primary students. This mini-lesson encourages students to view videos as well as read informational texts. Teachers should remind students that if they find conflicting infor-mation in the sources, they must check a third source to determine what information is correct. This mini-lesson prompts teachers to guide young readers of informational text to take notes so they recall the information they read/viewed from different sources. After this mini-lesson, students are encouraged to write a short paragraph comparing dolphins and sharks. The additional texts include information on natural disasters, another sea creature, and categorizing words, a topic not often found in informational texts.

DOI: 10.4324/9781003283478-3

The second mini-lesson gives teachers ideas on how young writers can organize information. Students know the alphabet and the mentor text *ABC insects* (2014) by

The American Museum of Natural History gives simple facts about 26 different insects. Young writers will find this an easy organizational pattern to follow.

Tomi dePaola's *The cloud book* (1975) demonstrates to young readers the importance of using technical vocabulary and giving concise definitions to explain the technical terms to the readers. This mini-lesson suggests that teachers develop mini-lessons based on students' background knowledge by sharing sections of the book that give new information to their students. The mini-lesson ends with teachers and students writing concise definitions for technical terms. The three additional texts demonstrate authors highlighting and defining technical terms in different sizes and colored fonts.

The fourth mini-lesson on sea turtles includes a short YouTube video that compliments the text. Both the video and text give a strong appeal to readers to protect sea turtles. It is clear to readers/viewers that humans are the cause of sea turtles becoming extinct. The other three titles also have strong appeal to readers to protect creatures that cannot protect themselves; the only voice they have are readers who will spring into action.

In the fifth mini-lesson teachers guide students as they focus on sentence fluency in informational texts. Many short, simple sentences in a text often do not show the relationship between pieces of information. In this mini-lesson teachers demonstrate that authors use both short and longer sentences to create fluent texts.

In the sixth mini-lesson, teachers introduce primary students to parentheses for the purpose of giving additional information to readers. In the mentor text *North American animals: Bald eagles* (2015), Bowman used parentheses to give measurements in English units. Two of the additional mentor texts demonstrate the use of commas in series, and the third additional text again demonstrates the use of parentheses.

In the seventh mini-lesson, teachers guide students to take notice of the details authors use to give the text eye appeal. In *Life cycle of a butterfly* (2019), Latchana Kenney used different colors for chapter titles and backgrounds. Inserted boxes share additional information. This type of format draws readers into the text. Teachers should encourage students to focus on eye appeal by using boxes and different colors for page numbers and technical terms.

Grade Level: Primary

Trait: Content

Genre: Informational

Mentor Text: *Dolphins and Sharks: Fact Tracker*

Author: Pope Osborne, M. & Pope Boyce, N.

Objective: "Write informative/explanatory texts in which they introduce a topic, use facts and definitions to develop points, and provide a concluding statement or section" (CCSS.ELA– Literacy.W.2.2).

This text has information that many books about dolphins and sharks do not have.

Procedure:

1. During your shared reading you do each day, read this entire informational book, sharing one chapter each day.
   a. After each chapter, have students share what they learned by asking them what was the most interesting fact they learned that they did not know before.
   b. As they dictate, write their comments on poster boards so you can display them in your Writing Center.
   c. In your Listening Center, each week have one of the websites that is shared on pages 112–113 so students can read and listen to more information about dolphins and sharks.
   d. Ask students to write what they learned on the poster boards.
2. After you have read the entire book, you are ready for this mini-lesson.
   a. Go back to the Table of Contents and the posters you created with the information.

    b. Invite students to look at the posters and write down, using Figure 3.1, the information from each chapter that interested them.

    c. Invite them to use their notes to write a short paragraph comparing and contrasting dolphins' and sharks' traits.

    d. Remind them to use information that is new to them.

    e. Remind students that a paragraph has only one topic.

5. Explain to students that taking notes on chapters is a good way to write research reports.

6. Additional Mentor Texts

    a. Osborne, W., & Pope Osborne, M. (2003). *Twisters and other terrible storms*. Random House. This Magic Tree House chapter book covers wind, clouds, rain, hurricanes, and blizzards. Each chapter has fascinating information written for early elementary students.

    b. Pope Osborne, M., & Pope Boyce, N. (2008). *Sea monsters*. Random House. This Magic Tree House chapter book covers information about the giant squid, dragon fish, and how sea creatures find food in the deep dark sea.

    c. Reynolds, P. (2018). *The word collector*. Orchard books. This mentor text demonstrates that informational texts can be about words. Reynolds categorizes words according to the number of syllables they have, the strength of words, and figures of speech.

Genre: Informational

Mentor Text: *Dolphins and Sharks: Fact Tracker*

Author: Pope Osborne, M. & Pope Boyce, N.

Information we learned from the book: notes from chapters

Chapter1: Oceans
Chapter 2: Dolphins
Chapter 3: Dolphin life
Chapter 4: Sharks
Chapter 5: Sharks as predators
Chapter 6: Shark attack!
Chapter 7: Saving dolphins and sharks

TRAIT: CONTENT
FIGURE 3.1

Grade Level: Primary

Trait: Organization

Genre: Informational

Mentor Text: *ABC Insects*

Author: The American Museum of Natural History

Objective: "Write information/explanatory texts in which they introduce a topic, use facts, and definitions to develop points, and provide a concluding statement or section" (CCSS.ELA-Literacy.W.2.7).

Procedure:

1. Flip through each page and ask open-ended questions about the organization of each double page.
   a. What did you notice about the format of each page?
      i. How is the book organized? Is it effective to organize the book according to the alphabet? Why or why not?
      ii. Why do they think "M." "N," "O," and "P" have different formats?
      iii. Are the color of letters, words, and backgrounds helpful in understanding the information?
      iv. Which is more effective, illustrations or photographs?
      v. Is there any other thing that caught your attention?
   b. Did you like the organization? If so, why? If not, how would you change it?
2. Read the "J," "K," and "L" information pages.
   a. Let students comment on the information.
   b. Is it interesting?
   c. Is it too detailed?
   d. Is there not enough information?

3. Discuss what topic besides insects could become an ABC book.
4. Discuss how they can use a camera to take photographs, and then with the help of an adult insert them in the text.
5. Pass out the templates for the double pages (See Figure 3.2) so students have a template to follow if they want to write their ABC informational book.
6. Additional Mentor Texts
   a. Herrington, L. M. (2015). *Turtles and tortoises*. Children's Press. The photographs and text concisely explain the differences between turtles and tortoises.
   b. Kras, S. L. (2010). *Koalas*. Capstone Press. This is a good mentor text to show young writers how to organize interesting facts about one particular creature. The book has four main facts that are used to create the chapters.
   c. Marsh, L. (2015). *Alligators and crocodiles*. National Geographic Kids. The detailed photographs and text give young children an understanding of the difference between these two creatures. Teachers can create a Venn diagram and encourage students to write a concise paragraph comparing and contrasting them.

Genre: Informational

Mentor Text: *ABC Insects*

Author/Illustrator: The American Museum of Natural History

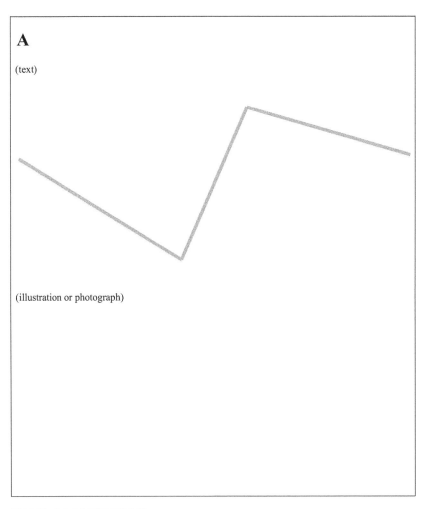

TRAIT: ORGANIZATION
FIGURE 3.2

B

(text)

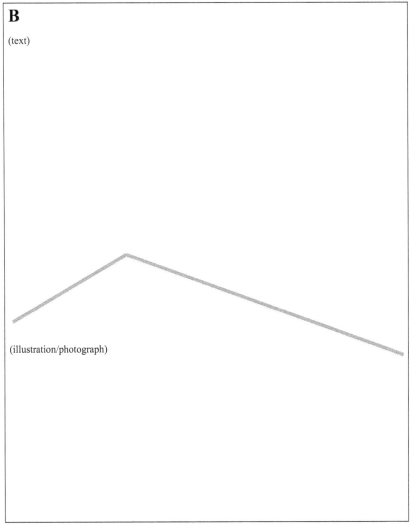

(illustration/photograph)

TRAIT: ORGANIZATION (CONTINUED)
FIGURE 3.2 (CONTINUED)

Grade Level: Primary

Trait: Word Choice

Genre: Informational

Mentor Text: *The Cloud Book*

Author/Illustrator: Tomie dePaola

Objective: "Write informative/explanatory texts in which they introduce a topic, use facts and definitions to develop points, and provide a concluding statement or section" (CCSS ELA– L.W 2.2).

Procedure:

1. Decide how much your students know about clouds before you read the entire book.
   a. If you have never studied clouds before, read only pages 1–11.
   b. If you have studied cirrus, cumulus, and stratus clouds, review the three types and begin reading on pages 12–17.
   c. Give students just enough new information that they will be able to pronounce the technical terms and give descriptions of clouds you introduce,
2. After you decide which pages to read, (e.g. the three main clouds) read only the pages that cover the new information.
   a. Then project page 8 to show students how dePaola italicized the technical names of the clouds.
   b. Also discuss how the last sentence on page 8, directs readers to the information that dePaola shared on the following pages.
   c. Project page 9 so students can view the text that italicizes *cirrus* and defines the technical term.

    d. Next, project page 10 and point out how dePaola again italicized *cumulus* so readers comprehend that cumulus is another type of cloud. Again dePaola used a clear explanation of cumulus clouds.

    e. Finally, project page 11 so students can view the text that italicizes *stratus* clouds.

    f. Ask students if dePaola describes stratus clouds in the same way he did cirrus and cumulus clouds.

3. Explain that when they write, they must do the following.
   a. Italicize the new word and give a short, concise definition so all readers can comprehend the new word.
   b. Illustrations must aid readers' comprehension.

4. Project Figure 3.3 so students can read it.
   a. Invite students to write a sentence, underlining the new words because writers underline words that computers italicize.
   b. They should give a short, concise definition. Work on writing concise definitions.

5. Additional Mentor Texts
   a. Bassier, E. (2020). *Dolphins*. Pop Books. This text has technical terms in bold print with explanations as part of the text. The Glossary includes the terms that are in bold print.
   b. Bowman, C. (2015). *North American animals: Bald eagles*. Bellwether Media. This text uses bold print to introduce readers to technical terms. The context of the text explains the terms.
   c. Thomson, S. L. (2006). *Amazing dolphins*. HarperCollins. The author adds in parenthesis the pronunciation of new terms. This is another feature young writers can include in their informational passages.

Genre: Informational

Mentor Text: *The Cloud Book*

Author/Illustrator: Tomie dePaola

1. Using the Internet, find pictures of a poodle and a lab dog. These two dogs are very different in size and appearance. Project the pictures so all students can see them. Cut and paste the following Internet addresses:

    www.istockphoto.com/search/2/image?phrase=poodle has some good pictures of poodles.

    https://pixabay.com/images/search/labrador/ has many pictures of labs.

2. With your help, have students dictate a short, concise definition of a poodle. Write it as the students dictate it. Review it, asking students if it is a concise definition.

3. With your help, have students dictate a short, concise definition of a lab. Write as your students dictate it. Review it, asking if it is a concise definition.

TRAIT: WORD CHOICE
FIGURE 3.3

Grade Level: Primary

Trait: Voice

Genre: Informational

Mentor Text: *Sea Turtles*

Author: Jared Siemens

Objective: "Introduce a topic, clearly, provide a general observation and focus, and group related information logically; include formatting (e.g., heading), illustrations, and multimedia when useful to aiding comprehension" (CCSS. ELA – Literacy.W.5.2a).

Procedure:

1. Read and discuss the entire book, showing the illustrations.
2. Go to www.av2books.com and share the video. Page 2 of the book has a code that you need to view the video.
   a. The beautiful video is only 1.35 minutes, and students will get to see sea turtles in their natural environment.
   b. The video ends with the same strong warning that is found on page 21 of the text: Sea turtles are in danger.
   c. After viewing the video that ends with the strong warning, reread page 21 and discuss with students all the items that kill sea turtles.
3. Teach students to understand that when they get information from different sources that they need to record from which source they learned the facts. You can teach them by completing Figure 3.4 with the students' input.
4. Display Figure 3.3 as a poster in the Writing Center so students can refer back to it.
5. This is a good book to use as a mentor text to encourage students to research other dangers found in the oceans that kill sea creatures.

6. **Additional Texts**
   a. Llewellyn, C. (2005). *Rainforest animals*. Sea-To-Sea. This easy to understand text. The last chapter "Animals in danger" alerts readers that people are a great danger to the animals that live in rainforests because people cut down the trees for new roads and farms. There is a website students can use to find out more about protecting forests and parks.
   b. Newman, P. (2017). *Sea otter heroes: The predators that saved an ecosystem*. This informational book looks at how sea otters are part of the ecosystem; therefore, they must be protected.
   c. Cousteau, P., & Hopkinson, D. (2016). *Follow the moon home: A tale of one idea, twenty kids, and a hundred sea turtles*. Chronicle Books. This informational book encourages children to become activists for saving sea turtles.

Mentor Text: *Sea Turtles*

Author: Jared Siemens

Researching and Recording Information from Two Sources

FACT: Dangers to Sea Turtles	Book Source: Siemens, J. (2022b). Sea Turtles	Video Source: www.av2books.com

GENRE: INFORMATIONAL
FIGURE 3.4

Grade Level: Primary
Trait: Sentence Fluency
Genre: Informational
Mentor Text: *Amazing Dolphins!*
Author/Illustrator: Sarah L. Thomson
Objective: "Produce, expand, and rearrange complete simple and compound sentences" (CCSS ELA-Literacy.L.2.2).

Procedure

1. The day before you teach this mini-lesson, read and discuss *Amazing dolphins!* to the large group.
   a. After reading the book, have the students share what they learned from the book.
   b. If students do not agree with a classmate's idea, ask the student who gave the idea to find the place in the book where they learned that information.
   c. On a poster board write the information that students share.
2. On the day of the mini-lesson, project Figure 3.5a and read it, making sure you also "read" the commas.
3. Engage students in open-ended questions so they focus on sentence fluency.
   a. How many sentences did the author use to tell readers for what humans use their mouths?
   b. How many sentences did the author use to tell readers for what dolphins use their mouths?
   c. Did the author use a different sentence to tell readers how dolphins breathe?
   d. Did the author write another sentence to let readers know how they make sounds?

    e. Point out to the students that in the first sentence the author used commas to list all the things humans use their mouths for.

    f. The author then used a short simple sentence to tell readers what dolphins use their mouths for.

    g. The author then uses a simple sentence with phrases to tell readers where the blowhole is on dolphins and what it does with the blowhole.

    h. Explain that when authors use short and longer sentences in a paragraph that makes good sentence fluency.

4. Project Figure 3.5b and ask students to write two sentences with the information that is given.

5. Have a few students read their sentences while classmates listen for sentence fluency.

6. **Additional Texts**

    a. dePaola, T. (1977). *The quicksand book*. Holiday House.

    b. dePaola, T. (1978). *The popcorn book*. Holiday House.

    c. dePaola, Y. (1979). *The kids' cat book*. Holiday House.

These three texts demonstrate sentence fluency. dePaola integrates simple, compound, and complex sentences with embedded phrases.

> **Genre:** Informational
>
> **Mentor Text:** *Amazing Dolphins!*
>
> **Author/Illustrator:** Sarah L. Thomson/The Wildlife Conservation Society

You use your mouth to breathe,
to eat, and to make sounds.
A dolphin uses its mouth to eat.
It uses the blowhole
On top of its head
To breathe and to make sounds.

FIGURE 3.5A

Create two sentences, using all the information.
George likes hot dogs.
George likes mustard on his hot dogs.
George does not like catsup on his hot dogs.
Juan likes tacos.
Juan likes soft shells.
Juan likes hamburger in his taco.
Juan likes taco sauce in his taco.
Juan likes onions in his taco.
Juan does not like green peppers in his taco.

FIGURE 3.5B

Grade Level: Primary

Trait: Conventions

Genre: Informational

Mentor Text: *North American Animals: Bald Eagles.*

Author: Chris Bowman

Objective: "Demonstrate command of the conventions of standard English capitalization, punctuation, and spelling when writing" (CCSS.ELA-Literacy.L.2.2).

Procedures:

1. The day before the mini-lesson, read and discuss *North American animals: Bald eagles.*
2. At the beginning of the mini-lesson project the sentence in the first part of Figure 3.6.
3. Point out how the author gave the English units in the body of the text and added the Metric units in parentheses.
   a. Discuss how the parentheses added additional information, keeping the sentence concise.
4. Project the two sentences in the last part of Figure 3.6 and discuss how the author used parentheses again to show the Metric units of meters and kilograms.
   a. Give students an opportunity to discuss how the Metric system has smaller numbers than the English units.
5. Ask students to think of other types of information authors may put into parentheses that give added information (e.g. definitions, similes), keeping the sentence concise.
6. Additional Mentor Texts
   a. De Medeiros, J. (2022). *Dolphins.* AV2 Books. This mentor text shows young students that not all series need to be single words; they also can be phrases.

Page 11 used the phrases: "how far away an object is, how large it is, and its general shape" (p. 11). The series keep authors from writing short, choppy sentences.

b. Murray, P. (2007). *Frogs*. The Child's World. This is a good mentor text to show young writers how authors set off series with commas. Page 23 has an example of a six-word series.

c. Siemens, J. (2022a). *Humpback whales*. AV2 books. This book has parentheses to show weight and height in Metric units. Pages 9, 15, and 17 have examples.

Genre: Informational

Mentor Text: *North American Animals: Bald Eagles.*

Author: Chris Bowman

Examples of ways to use parentheses to give readers added information.

"They are often 6 feet (1.8 meters) wide and 4 feet (1.2 meters) high" (Bowman, 2015, p. 11).

FIGURE 3.6 - FIRST PART

Examples of how to use parentheses to give readers added information.

"They are up to 3 feet (0.9 meters) tall. Most weigh about 14 pounds (6.4 kilograms)" (Bowman, 2015, p. 8).

FIGURE 3.6 - LAST PART

Grade Level: Primary

Trait: Presentation

Genre: Informational

Mentor Text: *Life Cycle of a Butterfly.*

Author: Latchana Kenney

Objective: "With guidance and support from adults, use a variety of digital tools to produce and publish writing, including in collaboration with peers" (CCSS.ELA-Literacy.W.2.6).

Procedure:

1. The day before you use this mentor text, read and discuss the information during shared reading.
2. Start the mini-lesson by sharing the Table of Contents just to review the topics of the text.
3. Turn to pages 4 and 5 and lead students in open-ended questions.
   a. What color print is the chapter number? Does that give eye appeal? Explain.
   b. What color print is the chapter title?
   c. On page 4, in the insert, what type of information is given to the readers?
   d. On page 5, what color is the box that has information about the photograph?
4. Turn to pages 8, 9, and 12.
   a. What do you notice about these boxes?
5. As you flip through the pages, comment on the beautiful photographs and how they help readers comprehend the text.
6. Invite students to brainstorm about topics they would like to photograph and what type of information they could include. Record their ideas on the table found in Figure 3.7.

7. Additional Mentor Texts
    a. De Medeiros, J. (2022). *Dolphins*. AV2 Books. This mentor text inserts the main photo in a geometric insert. Small boxes give additional information with additional smaller photographs.
    b. Siemens, J. (2022a). *Humpback whales*. AV2. This mentor text demonstrates how students can include a quiz at the end of the text. This is one way to review the main points. All the photographs are large to keep with the theme of how big these creatures are.
    c. Simon, S. (2015). *Frogs*. Harper/HarperCollins. The layout of this book has text dominating one side of the double page with large photographs supporting the text on the opposite page.

Trait: Presentation

Genre: Informational

Mentor Text: *Life Cycle of a Butterfly.*

Author: Latchana Kenney

Table to record ideas for informational texts with photographs

Topic/Photograph	Types of Information

GRADE LEVEL: PRIMARY
FIGURE 3.7

4

Informational Elementary Texts

Introduction

Chapter 4 begins with a mini-lesson based on murals found in San Diego. The mentor text *Maybe something beautiful: How art transformed a neighborhood* (2016) by Campoy and Howell is written in story form but relates the information about the Urban Art Trail in San Diego. The author notes at the end of the text give additional information. Elementary students do not often think that informational texts can be about murals found in their community. The mini-lesson encourages students to research and write about the murals they see in their town or city. The additional mentor texts include information about the first steam locomotive from Omaha to Sacramento, the invention of bubble gum, and the creator of the balloons seen in the Macy's parade in New York City. These mini-lessons give students unique content ideas for writing informational texts.

The second mini-lesson focuses on organization of informational text. The lesson is based on *Cheetahs* (Markert, 2007), which demonstrates the use of questions as chapter titles. Each chapter is only a double page, but the information answers the question. Two of the additional mentor texts also have questions as chapter titles. The third additional title is organized as a graphic text.

The third trait of the 6 + 1 Writing Traits is word choice. *Locomotive* (Floca, 2013) has ample examples of figures of speech, onomatopoeia, and technical terms. The beautiful illustrations

DOI: 10.4324/9781003283478-4

and poetic language demonstrate that informational texts can use figures of speech as well as give detailed information about a topic, in this lesson the steam engine. The three additional mentor texts include bold font or italics for technical vocabulary.

Endangered desert animals (Allgor, 2013) demonstrates how authors with marine biologists use strong language to appeal to readers to save endangered animals. Two of the additional mentor texts use photographs to show the beauty of these animals. The third additional text is in graphic form with a fish-like character making a strong appeal to readers not to put trash in oceans.

Sentence fluency is found in many informational texts. The mentor text *Bananas!* (Farmer, 1999) has ample examples of sentence fluency throughout the text. Many complex and compound-complex sentences are followed by short, simple sentences. After teachers analyze the sentence with students and encourage them to write with a mixture of sentence lengths, students will find their writing has more appeal to readers.

A good mentor text to demonstrate the sixth trait, conventions, is *Moonshot: The flight of Apollo 11* (Floca, 2009). Floca uses both dashes and ellipses. These are two conventions that students often ignore in their writing, and perhaps they do not understand their purpose when they come across them while reading. This sixth mini-lesson has open-ended questions that teachers can use to guide students in understanding how to properly use these conventions.

The seventh mini-lesson in Chapter 4 is on presentation. One informational text that has great visual appeal to elementary students is *Science comics: Coral reefs: Cities of the ocean* (Wicks, 2016). It is a graphic text, called a *science comic*, which appeals to many students. The open-ended questions given in the mini-lesson will guide students in discovering all the details that Wicks included to give the text visual appeal while sharing important information about coral reefs. The fish-like character gives readers detailed information about the reefs and how humans must help protect them. The three additional mentor texts are also classified as science comics.

Each mini-lesson should give young writers new ideas to incorporate into their writing.

Grade Level: Elementary

Trait: Content

Genre: Informational

Mentor Text: *Maybe Something Beautiful: How Art Transformed a Neighborhood*

Author: F. Isabel Campoy and Theresa Howell

Objective: "Use concrete words and phrases and sensory details to convey experiences and events precisely" (CCSS. LEA-Literacy.W.5.3.d).

Note: This unique informational book is told in story form; however, it gives information on the Urban Art Trail in San Diego, California. The author's notes give additional information.

Procedure:

1. After reading the picture book, turn back to the page where the muralist begins to paint. Lead the students in an open-ended discussion that will have them focus on how the author and illustrator use different colors throughout the text to aid in relating the content.
   a. Why did the author and illustrator use a double page and position the illustration sideways?
   b. Why did the author put the words "BAM! POW!" in large, orange font? What does that do for the readers' senses? How does that support the topic of the text?
   c. On the following page, why does the author put the text "THEN COME ON!" in large, purple font? What does that do for the readers' senses? How are the author and illustrator attempting to get readers to react to the various colors?
   d. On the page after that, what do the words "YOW-WEE!" in yellow do for the senses?

    e. On the third to last page, the authors and illustrator use a double page. How does the double-page layout complement the text "Wherever Mira and the man went, art followed like the string of a kite"? Discuss how it conveys the entire experience of painting a large mural.

2. Be sure to share the author's notes about the Urban Art Trail in San Diego.

3. After enjoying the book, invite students to think about murals that they see around their town or city.

    a. Record them in Figure 3.7.

    b. Invite students to contact their local art council or city council to explore who is the artist of the mural and if it was commissioned by a local organization or business.

4. Additional Mentor Text

    a. Floca, B. (2013). *Locomotive*. Atheneum Books for Young Readers. This mentor text with rhyme and poetic verse does not read like an informational text; however, it gives the history of the first steam power locomotive and its tracks from Omaha to Sacramento. It explains how steam engines work.

    b. McCarthy, M. (2010). *Pop! The invention of bubble gum.* A Paula Wiseman Book/Simon & Schuster Books for Young Readers. This mentor text relates how Walter Diemer worked years on inventing bubble gum with which people could pop bubbles. There are author notes about Walter Deimer at the end of the book. This fascinating book may grab the attention of students who are reluctant to read and write informational texts.

    c. Sweet, M. (2011). *Balloons over Broadway: The story of the puppeteer of Macy's Parade*. A Junior Library Guild Selection. This fascinating mentor text gives the history of the puppeteer who created helium balloons for the Thanksgiving Macy's Parade. The content includes information about the puppeteer Tony Sarg.

Genre: Informational

Mentor Text: *Maybe Something Beautiful: How Art Transformed a Neighborhood*

Authors: F. Isabel Campoy and Theresa Howell

Mural Topic Description	Location in Town/City

TRAIT: CONTENT
FIGURE 4.1

Grade Level: Elementary

Trait: Organization

Genre: Informational

Mentor Text: *Cheetahs*

Author/Illustrator: Jenny Markert

Objective: "Develop a topic with facts, definitions, concrete details, quotations, or other information and examples related to the topic" (CCSS.ELA-Literacy.W.5.2.b).

Note: This text is organized with a question as the chapter title, and the chapter gives the answer to the question. Each chapter is one question.

Procedure:

1. Begin by showing the students each page so they can see how the author organized the book on each double page. Lead them in open-ended questions so they focus on the organization of the text.
   a. Looking at the Table of Contents and titles of the chapters, what do you notice about the titles?
   b. Are questions effective for informational text? Why or why not? Explain your stance.
   c. What font for chapter titles did Markert use? Is that effective? Explain.
   d. Why do you think Markert used full-page photographs on the page opposite the text?
   e. Is the consistent layout helpful for readers to comprehend the text, or is it boring?
   f. Do the photographs clarify the text? Explain.
2. Read page 12 "What are Cheetahs' Claws Like?" so students know what specific information is shared in a chapter.

    a. Is the information in the large sidebar easy to comprehend?

    b. What type of details do the sidebars give?

    c. Does the fact that the caption of the photograph is on the opposite page of the photograph confuse readers? Explain.

    d. How do the page numbers reflect the information of the text?

    e. Why do you think the author separates the sections of each page with fine dotted lines?

3. Share the end of the text: Glossary, To Find Out More, and Index that includes notes about the author. Are these parts helpful, or would students not use them?

4. Let students discuss some possible topics they can research and unique layouts for the pages.

    a. Invite students to come to the board to draw a layout of a page.

5. Additional Mentor Texts:

    a. Wicks, M. (2016). Science comics: *Coral reefs: Cities of the ocean*. First Second. This science comic (organized with panels and one character as the narrator) can be used to show students that informational texts can be organized into panels with terse text to relate information to readers. The narrator is engaging as he (the fish) shares great details about the makeup of a coral reef.

    b. Murray, P. (2007). *Frogs*. The Child's World. Each double page is one chapter. Each chapter has text on one side with a full-page photograph on the opposite page. Each chapter includes a sidebar on the text page that has additional facts. At the bottom of the text page is italicized text that describes the photograph. This organization is used throughout the text.

    c. Siemens, J. (2022a). *Humpback whales*. AV2 Books. Each double page is a chapter in which the title is a large, colorful font. Each double page has main facts that support the chapter title with smaller inserts with facts.

Grade Level: Elementary

Trait: Word Choice

Genre: Informational

Mentor Text: *Locomotive*

Author/Illustrator: Brian Floca

Objective: "Use concrete words and phrases and sensory details to convey experiences and events precisely" (CCSS. ELA–Literacy-W.5.3.d).

Procedure:

1. After reading and discussing the information students learned about building the first railroad across the United States, discuss the style that Floca used to share the information. Use Figure 4.1 to record the discussion.
   a. Did he use any poetic form? If so, on what page?
   b. What are some vivid words he used?
   c. Did he use technical terms? If so, which words?
   d. Did he use any figurative language? If so, what are some examples?
2. Go back to the page that explains and shows how the locomotive passed through the Sierra Nevada mountain range and read from the book if possible so students can view the different fonts Floca used.
   a. Discuss the meanings of *summit, granite,* and *nitroglycerin*. Be sure students fully comprehend how hard granite is so they understand the danger the railroad workers endured when they used black powder and nitroglycerin.
   b. Discuss the onomatopoeia *boomed* and *chug-chug* and the font Floca used to represent the meaning of the words.

    c. Point out how Floca wrote *chug-chug* to represent the echo passengers heard in the tunnel.

3. Encourage students to use precise, concrete words when writing and to add onomatopoeia when appropriate to add meaning to the text.

4. Additional Mentor Texts

    a. Murray, P. (2007). *Frogs*. The Child's World. Murray prints technical terms in bold print to alert readers that these are technical words regarding frogs.

    b. Simon, S. (2015). *Frogs*. Harper/HarperCollins. Publishers. Simon used different color print when he introduces a different type of frog and used bold print when he explained technical terms. The Glossary lists technical terms with concise definitions.

    c. Mills, A. (2018). *The everything book of cats and kittens*. DK/Penguin Random House. Mills has one page for each of the general traits of cats and one page for the many different breeds of cats. Mills names and gives information on 42 different breeds of cats.

Genre: Informational

Mentor Text: *Locomotive*

Author/Illustrator: Brian Floca

4.2: Table to record discussion on word choice

Poetic Forms	Vivid Word Choice	Technical Terms	Figure of Speech

TRAIT: WORD CHOICE
FIGURE 4.2

Grade Level: Elementary
Trait: Voice
Genre: Informational
Mentor Text: *Endangered Desert Animals*
Author / Illustrator: Marie Allgor
Objective: "Provide a concluding statement or section related to the information or explanation presented" (CCSS. ELA-Literacy.W.5.2.e).

Procedure:

1. Turn to the Table of Contents and read the chapter titles.
2. Read pages 10–11, pointing out that in the United States the desert tortoise is endangered.
3. Read pages 20–21 about the desert tortoise since it is a creature that lives in the United States. Lead students in discussion with these questions. Be sure to read the captions of each photo.
   a. What is the ideal habitat for desert tortoises?
   b. What specific facts does the author give about the declining numbers of desert tortoises?
   c. What or who is a danger to the desert tortoise?
4. Read page 22 "Save the desert's animals." Lead students in the following discussion.
   a. What is helping to save the desert's animals?
   b. What can humans do?
   c. The author voiced the plea that it is our job to help these creatures. What can we do?
   d. Post the website, given on the last page, on a poster in your Writing Center and encourage students to view it, and have them add to the poster as found in Figure 4.2.
5. Additional Mentor Text

a. Lockwood, S. (2006). *Sea turtles*. The Child's World. Lockwood shares information about sea turtles in their natural habitat. Chapter 5 "Humans and sea turtles" explains that for years humans hunted sea turtles and brought the numbers down so that there is a threat to their survival today. Facts make it clear to readers how much the sea turtles are in danger. Lockwood shares some of the many dangers to turtles, including humans. Toward the end of the chapter, she gives the goals of conservationists.

b. Markert, J. (2007). *Elephants*. The Child's World. Markert gives a strong voice throughout the book about the danger that elephants face and what humans can do to protect them. The beautiful photographs of elephants in their natural habitat are one way of convincing readers that these creatures must be protected.

c. Wicks, M. (2016). *Science comics coral reefs, cities of the ocean*. First Second. One excellent, engaging book for students who love graphic informational texts is this one by Maris Wicks who is a marine biologist and has studied coral reefs for 15 years. Chapter 5 of *Coral reefs* shares all the things that damage not only coral reefs but also other animals on land and sea. You can point students to Chapter 5 to read how Wicks gives a strong voice to the text.

Trait: Voice

Genre: Informational

Mentor Text: *Endangered Desert Animals*

Author: Marie Allgor

Find the website as listed on the Internet, and have students add information they find about endangered animals and what action they can take to protect them.

Website: www.powerkidslinks.com/sea/desert

Facts About Endangered Creatures	What Action Humans Can Take to Protect Them

FIGURE 4.3

Grade Level: Elementary

Trait: Sentence Fluency

Genre: Informational

Mentor Text: *Bananas!*

Author: Jacqueline Farmer

Objective: "Demonstrate command of the conventions of standard English capitalization, punctuation, and spelling when writing" (CCSS ELA-Literacy. L5.2).

Bananas has many examples of sentence fluency. You can use others than the following suggested one.

Procedure:

1. First read Example A found in Figure 4.3 and lead students in the following discussion.
   a. Does this sound like fluent writing? Explain.
   b. What would you do to make it fluent?
2. Then project Example B and ask students if they think that sounds like fluent writing and lead them in the following discussion.
   a. What type of sentence is it? Compound? Complex? Compound-complex? Simple?
   b. What type of clause begins the sentence?
   c. What type of clause follows the first clause?
   d. Are there any types of phrases? If so, what are they?
   e. What type of phrase or clause ends the sentence?
3. For an example to demonstrate to students how a series in a sentence creates a more fluid sentence than one with many simple sentences, use Examples C and D.
   a. What did you notice about Example C?
   b. Ask a student to read it and to comment on its fluency.
   d. Then project Example D and ask a student to read and comment on its fluency.

e. Analyze the series in the sentence found in Example D and discuss how using a series can create sentence fluency.
4. Project Example E and ask students to create a sentence that is fluent.
5. Have students share their sentences.
6. Additional Mentor Texts
   a. Gerstein, M. (2003). *The man who walked between the towers*. Roaring Brook Press. Gerstein uses a variety of simple, compound, and compound-complex sentences to indicate the pace Philippe took when stepping on and walking across the tight wire.
   b. Simon, S. (2015). *Frogs*. Harper/HarperCollins. Publishers. Simon uses series and embedded phrases to make his writing fluent. There are many examples, but if you want to use only one example, read page 23.
   c. George, M. (2007). *Bats*. The Child's World. George includes questions within a paragraph and then answers with sentences with embedded phrases and various types of clauses.

Genre: Informational

Mentor Text: *Bananas!*

Author: Jacqueline Farmer

EXAMPLE A

Bananas increase energy. Bananas contain amino acids. Amino acid is called tryptophan. Tryptophan makes people sleepy.

EXAMPLE B

"Even though bananas are known to increase energy, they also contain an amino acid, called tryptophan, that is thought to make people sleepy" (Farmer, 1999).

EXAMPLE C

Americans first peeled the fruit. Then they laid it on a plate. Next they cut it into small pieces. They used a fruit knife to cut it into small pieces. Finally they ate it. They ate it with a fruit fork.

EXAMPLE D

"Americans were told to peel the fruit, lay it on a plate, cut it into small pieces with a fruit knife, and eat it with a fruit fork" (Farmer, 1999).

EXAMPLE E

One banana contains lots of Vitamin B6. Vitamin B6 strengthens red blood cells. One banana also contains Vitamin C. Vitamin C keeps the body's organs healthy (Farmer, 1999).

TRAIT: SENTENCE FLUENCY
FIGURE 4.4

Grade Level: Elementary

Trait: Conventions

Genre: Informational

Mentor Text: *Moonshot: The Flight of Apollo 11*

Author: Brian Floca

Objective: "Demonstrate command of the conventions of standard English capitalization, punctuation, and spelling when writing" (CCSS ELA – Literacy.L5.2).

Procedure:

1. After reading and discussing *Moonshot,* project Figure 4.4 so all students can see it.
2. Analyze Floca's sentence structure by leading students in open-ended questions about the conventions that he used.
   a. Why are *Columbia* and *Eagle* capitalized?
   b. Why is there a comma after the word *space*?
   c. What type of phrase is *a monster of a machine?*
   d. What figure of speech did Floca use to help readers comprehend how huge the two spaceships are even though in the previous sentence Floca stated that they were *small*?
   e. Why did Floca use a colon after the word *machine*?
   f. What follows the colon?
   g. Did you notice anything about the series? Is the list single nouns?
   h. How did Floca describe *tower, valves, pipes*, and *engines*?
   i. Where did he place the adjectives?
   j. What follows the dash?
   k. What did Floca do to aid readers in comprehending that this "monster of a machine" is "the mighty, massive Saturn V"?

3. If time permits or if you think students would benefit from your leading them in placing a dash in a sentence, project the next paragraph (from the text) without any punctuation and have students decide where the commas and dash belong.

4. Add punctuation and capitalization "Practice Paragraph" (Figure 4.5) with the class.

5. Additional Mentor Texts

    a. Floca, B. (2013). *The locomotive*. A Richard Jackson Book/Atheneum Books for Young Readers. Throughout this book, Floca uses dashes and ellipses; one good page to use is the fourth and third to last pages.

    b. Sweet, M. (2011). *Balloons over Broadway: The story of the puppeteer of Macy's Parade*. A Junior Library Guild Selection. On the last page of text, Sweet used the dash to set off an appositive with embedded phrases.

    c. Wicks, M. (2016). *Science comics: Coral reefs: Cities of the ocean*. First Second. Using the last panel on page 97 and the first panel on page 98, teachers can demonstrate how authors use ellipses before a series; it also depicts how commas are used to separate items in a series.

Genre: Informational

Mentor Text: *Moonshot: The Flight of Apollo 11*

Author: Brian Floca

"Their two small spaceships are

Columbia and *Eagle*.

. . . that will lift them into space,

a monster of a machine:

it stands thirty stories,

it weighs six million pounds,

a tower full of fuel and fire

and valves and pipes and engines,

too big to believe, but built to fly –

the mighty, massive Saturn V" (Floca, 2009, fifth page of text).

PRACTICE PARAGRAPH

"The astronauts squeeze in

to *columbia's* sideways seats

lying on their back

facing toward the sky

neil armstrong on the left

michael collins on the right" (Floca, 2009).

TRAIT: CONVENTIONS
FIGURE 4.5

Grade Level: Elementary

Trait: Presentation

Genre: Informational

Mentor Text: *Science Comics: Coral Reefs: Cities of the Ocean.*

Author: Maris Wicks

Objective: "Introduce a topic, clearly, provide a general observation and focus, and group related information logically; include formatting, illustrations, and multimedia when useful to aiding comprehension" (CCSS.ELA-Literacy.W.2.a).

If your school library does not have this book, check your community library. If you cannot find it in either place, I suggest you order it to add to your classroom library. It is a graphic informational text and is very engaging.

Procedure:

1. Project page 2 and lead students in open-ended questions.
   a. What is the author doing in the first five panels?
   b. What does he do in the sixth panel?
   c. Does the format get readers' attention?
2. Project page 3 and ask some more open-ended questions.
   a. Is the format a unique way to introduce an informational book? Why or why not?
   b. Is the bottom panel a good position for the chapter title? Explain.
   c. Turn to the pages that include each chapter title (pp. 16, 30, 68, and 83).
   d. Which format is most helpful to readers? Explain.
3. Project page 4 and discuss the differently sized panels.
   a. Why do you think the author used the different sizes?
   b. What other formatting could the author have used that would be most helpful for readers to comprehend the text?

4. Project page 5 and discuss the effective formatting on this page.
5. Project page 6 and lead students in open-ended questions.
   a. What do you notice about the size of each panel?
   b. What do you notice about the use of bubbles?
   c. Are the bubbles helpful to readers to comprehend the text?
6. Give students time to comment on the effectiveness of using comic strip formatting to share information. Be sure to have them give reasons for their stance.
7. Pass out Figure 4.6 and project it so all students can see it.
   a. Invite them to comment on the formatting of each page; be sure to comment on panel sizes, placement of chapter titles, illustrations, bubbles, and lack of bubbles.
   b. Encourage students to keep notes and to consider writing an informational text using comic strip formatting.
8. Additional Mentor Texts
   a. Flood, J. (2018). *Science comics: Sharks: Nature's perfect hunter.* First Second. The information about sharks' physical makeup and their environment is told in comics. However, there is a strong warning about what kills sharks and how humans need to work to protect them.
   b. Hircsh, A. (2017). *Science comics: Dogs: From predator to protector.* First Second. The information about dogs' physical makeup and the environment is told in comics. These illustrations are not as detailed as the sharks and whales comics.
   c. Zakroff, C. (2021). *Science comics: Whales: Diving into the unknown.* First Second. The information about whales' physical makeup and their environment is told in comics. The comics show how marine biologists study whales in their natural habitat to understand how to protect their habitat. There is a warning to readers that humans need to work to protect the whales' environment.

Trait: Voice

Mentor Text: *Science Comics: Coral Reefs: Cities of the Ocean.*

Author: Maris Wicks

Features	*Comments*
Chapter title placement	
Panel Sizes	
Bubbles	
Use of character (fish) to give information	
Illustrations	

GENRE: INFORMATIONAL
FIGURE 4.6

5

Primary Poetry

Introduction

Many of the featured poems in this chapter can be found in anthologies and on the Internet. I included the website of most of the poems just in case teachers cannot find the books mentioned in Chapter 5. Because websites readily change, I suggest that teachers use the title of the poem as their search word as most poems can be found using that technique.

Poems can be about any topic, as demonstrated in the first lesson of Chapter 5. The mentor poem "What is yellow?" is highlighted because primary students have background knowledge about the color of objects. As teachers guide students through the open-ended questions in this mini-lesson, children will recognize that the poet mentioned ordinary yellow objects and the feeling that yellow gives her. Each of the additional mentor texts suggests a wide variety of topics – rockets, nature, and mermaids.

One way to organize a collection of poems is by writing a poem for each letter of the alphabet. One of Steven Schnur's acrostic alphabet books is highlighted to demonstrate to young writers that a collection of poems can be centered on the alphabet. Guiding students through the open-ended discussion will build students' confidence in writing poems. The additional mentor texts are organized around acrostic poems about African animals, punctuation marks, and acrostic poems about winter.

DOI: 10.4324/9781003283478-5

Many poems can be used to demonstrate how poets incorporate the third trait, word choice. Poets use alliteration, onomatopoeia, personification, similes, metaphors, and other forms of figurative language to give readers vivid images in their minds. Primary students understand alliteration because they work with initial sounds of letters. Thus, I selected "The whales off Wales" (Kennedy, 1975) found in *Book of animal poetry* (National Geographic, 2012) because it has multiple examples of alliteration with other vivid word choices.

Won Ton and Chopstick: A cat and dog tale told in haiku (Warlaw, 2015) demonstrates the fourth writing trait, voice. This unique book of haikus tells a story of Won Ton, the cat, who is totally upset when Chopstick, the dog, joins the family. Won Ton's tone of voice changes, however, when Chopstick meets a skunk. One of the additional mentor texts, *Dogku* (Clements, 2007), is another story told in a series of haiku poems. The dog uses a strong voice as he makes it known to the family that he wants to stay with them. The other two additional poems that demonstrate how poets use a strong voice are concrete poems: a football lamenting that no one cheers when it makes a move and a snowman's anger because no one gives him a hat when he is left out in the cold.

The fifth trait of sentence fluency is demonstrated in poems that are longer than haikus. "Our tree," the mentor poem, demonstrates how poets use longer sentences with embedded phrases interspersed with short simple sentences.

Often teachers attempt to teach students how to use commas in their poems. However, the featured mentor poem demonstrates the use of dialogue with exclamation marks. Having different students read the parts of Mirror and Queen will demonstrate the unique effect of quotation marks and exclamation marks in poems. The other mentor poems also feature dialogue with question marks.

There are a wide variety of ways to present poems so that they have visual appeal. I have chosen concrete poems to demonstrate to students that putting poems into the shape of their topic helps readers guess the topic before they read it. Simple shapes are a must for primary students; the featured mentor poem and the additional mentor poems are simple shapes.

Grade Level: Primary

Trait: Content

Genre: Poetry

Mentor Text: "What is Yellow?" in *Hailstones and Halibut Bones*

Author: Mary O'Neill

Objective: "Describe how words and phrases (e.g. regular beats, alliteration, rhymes, repeated lines) supply rhythm and meaning in a story, poem, or song" (CCSS.ELA-Literacy. RF.2.4).

The poem can also be found at the following site by scrolling down to "What is yellow?" Copy and paste the address in the URL bar.

I chose the topic of colors because young children have knowledge of what colors different objects are.

www.wadlin.com/hailstones.htm

Procedure:

1. Read the entire poem, the second to last poem in the book, but focus and discuss only the first six lines of the poem. Lead students in an open-ended question.
   a. What is the mood of this poem?
   b. Why did the poet list *egg yolks, canaries,* and *daffodils* as yellow objects?
2. Project the first six lines from the website and use open-ended questions for class discussion.
   a. What did you notice about each line?
   b. Why do you think the poet said that yellow is the "feeling of fun"?
   c. Is yellow a feeling of fun for you? Explain.
   d. Do any of the lines rhyme? If so, which ones?

    e. What do you think about all the lines that do not rhyme?

    f. Is there any punctuation at the end of the lines?

3. Discuss how the poet created a poem by listing items that are yellow. Encourage them to do the same.

4. Begin a class poem by projecting Figure 5.1 "What is green?" and ask students to give some ideas for lines.

5. Invite students to write a poem about their favorite color and give the title "What is (favorite color)?"

6. Additional Mentor Texts

    a. Cooling, W. (2010). *All the wild wonders: Poems of our earth*. Francis Lincoln Children's Books. These poems are about our beautiful world and how we must save it from all the rubbish around us. Encourage students to write a poem about any part of nature.

    b. Portis, A. (2020). *A new green day*. Neal Portis Books. This collection of poems is about the beautiful things that surround us. Some poems are riddles that take readers through a day, a night, and back again to day. Students can consider writing riddles as a poem.

    c. Stansfield, L. (2019). *Poems out loud: First poems to read and perform*. Ladybird. This collection of poems covers all topics from mermaids to rockets. Some are like hip-hop rhymes. This is a great book to demonstrate that poems can be about any topic.

Genre: Poetry

Mentor Text: "What is Yellow?" in *Hailstones and Halibut Bones*

Author: Mary O'Neill

CLASS POEM

What is green?

Green is _____

TRAIT: CONTENT
FIGURE 5.1

Grade Level: Primary

Trait: Organization

Genre: Poetry

Mentor Text: "Picnic" in *Summer: An Alphabet Acrostic*

Author: Steven Schnur

Objective: "With guidance and support from adults, produce writing in which the development and organization are appropriate to task and purpose" (CCSS.ELA-Literacy.W.3.4).

This book and Schnur's other season acrostic books are good ones to use to introduce students to acrostic poems because the organization is easy to understand.

Procedure:

1. Hold the book so all students can see the pages.
2. Flip through the first four or five poems, asking open-ended questions.
   a. What did you notice about the beginning of each poem?
   b. Is that a good way to organize a book of poems? Why or why not?
3. Explain that the entire book is organized according to the alphabet.
   a. Read the "Picnic" poem and lead students in an open-ended discussion.
   b. Do they like going on a picnic? Explain.
   c. What kind of food do you like to take on a picnic?
   d. What other items do you take on a picnic?
   e. What does the first letter of each line spell?
   f. Make sure they recognize that the poet used bold font for the first letter of each line.
4. Pass out Figure 5.2 and project one so all students can see it.

5. Brainstorm with the class about possible topics they could choose for an acrostic alphabet poem book. If you have recently studied a theme, such as sea creatures or the rainforest, suggest one of those topics.
6. Additional Mentor Texts
   a. Bennett Hopkins, L. (2018). *A bunch of punctuation*. Wordsong. Each poem is about a punctuation mark (e.g. exclamation, period, comma). The poems will give students other ideas for using punctuation marks as a way to organize poems.
   b. Harley, A. (2009). *African acrostic: A word in edgeways*. Candlewick Press. These poems are organized on various African animals. Not all the poems have the name of the animal going downward; some poems have the traits of the animals going downward.
   c. Schnur, S. (2002). *Winter: An alphabet acrostic*. Clarion Books. These poems are based on winter and organized by the alphabet.

Trait: Organization

Genre: Poetry

Mentor Text: "Picnic" in *Summer: An Alphabet Acrostic*

Author: Steven Schnur

Ideas for Acrostic Poems

Name: _____

Possible Topics/Organization	Possible Poem Titles
Sea Creatures	
Rain Forest	

FIGURE 5.2

Grade Level: Primary
Trait: Word Choice
Genre: Poetry
Mentor Text: "The Whales Off Wales" (p. 28) in *Book of Animal Poetry* or this Website: https://studylib.net/doc/8142844/second-grade-poetry-collection-2
Author: X. J. Kennedy
Objective: "Describe how words and phrases supply rhythm and meaning in a story, poem, or song" (CCSS.ELA-LR.2.4).

Note: If your school or community library does not have the book, you can copy and paste the address into the URL to read the poem. |

Procedure:

1. Using the Internet, show a short video of a whale so students understand how big they are and where they live.
2. Project the poem from the poetry book or from the website. Be sure all students can see it.
   a. Read the verse of the poem and lead students in open-ended questions.
      i. What do you notice about the initial letter of many of the words?
      ii. What is that called when a number of words begin with the same letter?
      iii. What do you think *walloping tails whacking waves* sound like?
      iv. Why do you think the poet says that they snore on a watery floor?
      v. Why do you think the poet thinks that whales wear wet woolen nightcaps?

    b. Read with expression the second stanza and ask opened-ended questions.
      i. Do you notice alliteration in the second verse?
      ii. Do any word rhyme in the second verse?

3. Ask students to stand up and pantomime whales gliding through the water.
    a. Is a glide a smooth movement?
    b. Is it easy to glide through water?

4. Ask students what words they thought were really descriptive that helped them visualize whales in the water. Record their answers on Figure 5.3 poster so they can use these words in their writing.

5. Project the beginning lines found in Figure 5.3 and ask students to think of alliteration and vivid words to finish the lines.

6. Additional Mentor Texts
    a. Bennett, J. (1987). *Noisy poems.* Oxford University Press. This collection of poems has many examples of onomatopoeia. "Jazz-Man" is one example.
    b. Schenk de Regniers, B., Moore, E., Michaels White, M., & Carr, J. (Eds.). (1988). *Sing a song of popcorn.* Scholastic. This collection of poems has many poems with excellent word choice. One recommendation is found on page 90. It is "Here comes the band."
    c. Sidman, J. (2009). *Red sings from treetops: A year in colors.* Houghton Mifflin Books for Children. This text is filled with vivid word images; many are similes and metaphors.

Mentor Text: "The Whales Off Wales" (p. 28) in *Book of Animal Poetry* or this Website: https://studylib.net/doc/8142844/second-grade-poetry-collection-2

Author: X. J. Kennedy

Vivid Words Used in "The whales off Wales"

Class' Poem with Alliteration

With the students' help, complete the following lines, using vivid words.

1. The elephant _____

2. The monkeys _____

3. The baby kitten _____

GENRE: POETRY
FIGURE 5.3

Grade Level: Primary

Trait: Voice

Genre: Poetry

Mentor Text: *Won Ton and Chopstick: A Cat and Dog Tale Told in Haiku*

Author: Lee Wardlaw

Objective: "Describe how words and phrases supply rhythm and meaning in a story, poem, or song" (CCSS Reading for Literature Standards 2.4).

Procedure

1. Read the short title: *Won Ton and Chopstick*, showing the book cover.
2. Ask students open-ended questions to get them to predict the book's content.
   a. Judging by the picture, whom do they think is Won Ton and who is Chopstick? Explain.
   b. Do you think the cat and dog are friends? Why or why not?
3. Read the first page and lead students in open-ended questions.
   a. Who is telling the story? How can you tell?
   b. Do you think the cat is a happy cat? Why or why not?
4. Read the second poem and discuss the following:
   a. What does the question: "Who dares disturb my beauty snooze?" tell you about the cat's personality?
   b. Does the cat appear to be agitated? Explain your stance.
5. Read the third poem and lead students in open-ended questions.
   a. The poet used the word *proper*. What does that tell you about the cat?

    b. Looking at the toys in the picture, who do you think is coming?

6. Read the fourth poem, emphasizing the words *curious* and *never*.

    a. Ask the class what these two words tell you about the cat's attitude.

7. Read the fifth poem, pausing at the two ellipses and emphasizing the word *FREEZE!* Then lead the students in the following discussion:

    a. How does the cat feel as it approaches the open door?

    b. What does the line: "My eyes full of DOOM!" tell us about the cat?

8. Read the sixth and seventh haikus

    a. Ask students to comment on what is happening. (Students will need to be able to see the pictures in order to fully comprehend what is happening.)

    b. Discuss how the cat may have said: "Puthimoutputhim outputhimoutputhim – wait!"

    c. What more does that tell readers about the cat?

9. Read the next page "Naming" as if you have the attitude of the cat. You want them to understand that the poet gives Cat a strong voice!

10. Read the rest of the story.

    a. Ask students, "When does Cat change his attitude about the dog? How can you tell?"

    b. Be sure to discuss any words that are unfamiliar to the students (e.g. *compelling, banishment, lament*).

11. After reading and discussing the entire story, making sure you have emphasized how the poet gives a strong voice to Cat, go back to the beginning and explain how the poet used haiku to tell this story.

12. Go back to the page in which Dog is chasing after the stunk.

    a. Invite students to give you some ideas about what the dog may be thinking at the time. Encourage them to give the dog a strong voice.

    b. Write down the students' ideas so all students can read them.

  c. Then see if your students can help you put those ideas into a haiku. Complete Figure 5.4.

  d. Display the class' haiku near your writing center so students can refer to it when they want to write a haiku in which the character has a strong voice.

13. Additional Mentor Texts

  a. Clements, A. (2007). *Dogku*. Simon & Schuster Books for Young Readers. This is another story told in a series of haiku poems. There is a strong voice for the dog to remain with this family who has three children who love the dog Mooch.

  b. Cleary, B. (2015b). BRRRR. In *Ode to commode: Concrete poems*. Milbrook Press. The snowman compliments the children for adding the coal for his eyes and a carrot for his nose, but he is totally upset that they gave him only a scarf and a hat in the deep winter cold.

  c. Cleary, B. (2015d). What about me? In *Ode to commode: Concrete poems*. Milbrook Press. The football is lamenting that the kickers, receivers, and running backs get cheers when they make their moves; however, the crowd never cheers for the football.

> **Mentor Text:** Won Ton and Chopstick: A Cat and Dog Tale Told in Haiku
>
> **Author:** Lee Wardlaw

In the table, record students' ideas about Dog's attitude when he is chasing after the skunk; encourage students to use words that will tell readers that Dog has a strong voice/opinion.

After recording some ideas, have students (with your guidance) write a haiku, giving Dog a strong voice.

Students' Original Thoughts	Revisions with Vivid Words and Five or Seven Syllables

Class Haiku

Five syllables _____

Seven syllables _____

Five syllables _____

GENRE: POETRY
FIGURE 5.4

Grade Level: Primary

Trait: Sentence Fluency

Genre: Poetry

Mentor Text: "Our Tree" in *Sing a Song of Popcorn*

Selected by: Marchette Chute (p. 27)

Objective: "Produce, expand, and rearrange complete simple and compound sentences" (CCSS ELA-Literacy. L.2.1.e).

"Our tree" can also be found on this website by copying and pasting the following in the URL.

www.poemhunter.com/poem/our-tree/

Procedure:

1. Lead students in guided questions so they understand what sentence fluency is.
   a. After stopping after the first line that ends in a comma, ask if this thought let readers know what season it is.
   b. Is it a complete sentence?
   c. Do readers know what happens when spring comes?
2. Read the second clause.
   a. Do readers know now what happens in spring?
   b. Point out that the poet used a comma at the end of the line instead of a period.
   c. When you come to a comma, do you come to a complete stop or do you take just a little pause?
3. Read the third line that is an incomplete sentence.
   a. Do you know what happens when a bird sits on a branch?
4. Read the last line so students can hear that it is a complete thought/sentence.

5. Reread the first verse, inviting students to listen to the fluency of the first verse.
6. Project the entire first verse, pausing at the commas, not stopping.
7. Point out the punctuation the poet used to make a long compound-complex sentence.
   a. Explain that combining thoughts and using the correct punctuation make for good "sentence fluency."
   b. You can write with fluency, just like you can read with fluency.
8. Project the short, choppy sentences found in Figure 5.5.
   a. Read it, stopping for each period.
   b. Ask students if that sounds very fluent.
   c. How can we make it a good fluent sentence?
9. Additional Mentor Poems
   a. Schenk de Regniers, B., Michaels White, M., & Carr, J. (Eds.). (1988). *Sing a song of popcorn*. Scholastic. "The old wife and the ghost" by James Reeve has many examples of fluent sentences. Some are long and interspersed with short, simple sentences.
   b. Sidman, J. (2009). *Red sings from treetops: A year in colors*. Houghton Mifflin Books for Children. One section that is good to use for sentence fluency and that primary students can comprehend is the "White" poem in spring (it is on page 5 of the text). It also has very vivid word choice.
   c. Schenk de Regniers, B., Michaels White, M., & Carr, J. (Eds.). (1988). *Sing a song of popcorn*. Scholastic. Each of the three verses of "Until I saw the sea" (Moore, 1988, p. 115) is one long fluent sentence. This poem demonstrates how students can write one sentence and put it into poetic form.

> **Genre:** Poetry
>
> **Mentor Text:** "Our Tree" in *Sing a Song of Popcorn*
>
> **Poet:** Marchette Chute (p. 27)

Project the following so all students can read it.

Ask a student to read it to the class.

Ask the student what it sounds like.

If students agree that it is choppy, rewrite it so it is a fluent sentence.

It is spring.

I see birds.

They are sitting on branches.

They are singing.

They are small.

They are yellow and black.

TRAIT: SENTENCE FLUENCY
FIGURE 5.5

Grade Level: Primary

Trait: Conventions

Genre: Poetry

Mentor Text: "Ickle Me, Pickle Me, Tickle Me Too" Found in *Where the Sidewalk Ends* (pp. 16–17) or at https://genius.com/Shel-silverstein-ickle-me-pickle-me-tickle-me-too-annotated

Author: Shel Silverstein (1974a)

Objective: "Demonstrate command of the conventions of standard English capitalization, punctuation, and spelling when writing" (CCSS.ELA-Literacy.L.2.2).

To access this website, copy and paste the website into the URL bar.

https://genius.com/Shel-silverstein-ickle-me-pickle-me-tickle-me-too-annotated

Procedure:

1. Project the poem so all can see, using either the book or the website.
2. Read the poem, using expression (e.g. using different voices for each character) and gestures (e.g. flap arms like a flying shoe), as shown through the punctuation, so students comprehend the humor in the poem.
3. Reread stanza one, leading students in open-ended questions about the punctuation marks.
   a. What are these marks called?
   b. What do they tell readers?
   c. What is this mark at the end of each speaker's quote?
   d. What do exclamation marks tell readers?
   e. Do you think the three characters were excited about flying in a shoe? Explain your answer.

    f. What does Silverstein do when a different speaker begins to talk?
4. Reread stanza three.
    a. Use the same voices for each character that you used in stanza one.
    b. Point out how again Silverstein used quotation marks with exclamation marks for each character.
5. Project Figure 5.6 so all can see.
    a. Invite a student to come up and circle the exclamation marks in red.
    b. Invite another student to come up and circle the quotation marks in blue. Be sure they circle the beginning and ending quotation marks.
6. Discuss how writing so characters are speaking in a poem makes the poem more interesting.
7. Project the poem starter found in Figure 5.6.
8. Invite students to write what each turtle might say to each other.
9. Additional Mentor Texts with Direct Quotes
    a. Prelutsky, J. (1988). "The spaghetti nut" (p. 109) in Schenk de Regniers, B., Michaels White, M., & Carr, J. (Eds.). (1988). *Sing a song of popcorn*. Scholastic. This is another poem to demonstrate to students the use of quotation marks and how direct quotes in a poem make a poem interesting.
    b. Sandburg, C. (1988). "We must be polite" (p. 96) in Schenk de Regniers, B., Michaels White, M., & Carr, J. (Eds.). (1988). *Sing a song of popcorn*. Scholastic. This mentor poem demonstrates how questions can be placed in a poem.
    c. Silverstein, S. (1974b). "Snowman" (p. 65) in *Where the sidewalk ends*. HarperCollins. This mentor poem has a snowman and robin talking back and forth. The poem demonstrates to students how poets use quotation marks with commas and periods. No exclamation marks are needed.

> **Mentor Text:** "Ickle Me, Pickle Me, Tickle Me Too" Found in *Where the Sidewalk Ends* (p. 16–17) or at https://genius.com/Shel-silverstein-ickle-me-pickle-me-tickle-me-too-annotated
>
> **Author:** Shel Silverstein

Project the following to draw attention to quotation marks and exclamation marks.

"Hold on to your hat!" Mother screamed!

"Oh my! Oh yeah! It flew away!" Charlie beamed.

Class Poem:

Invite students to dictate lines of what the turtles may be saying to each other.

Adventure of three turtles

Starter poem by Beverly A. DeVries

Murtle Turtle, Lurtle Turtle, and Rurtle Turtle stood at the edge of a lake.

A blue bottom boat

came chugging by

and stopped near Turtle Inn.

Murtle Turtle exclaimed, "_____

Lurtle Turtle shouted, "_____

Rurtle Turtle screamed, "_____

GENRE: POETRY
FIGURE 5.6

Grade Level: Primary

Trait: Presentation

Genre: Poetry

Mentor Text: "All Wet" (p. 25) in *Ode to a Commode: Concrete Poems.*

Author: Brian Cleary (2015a)

Objective: "With guidance and support from adults, use a variety of digital tools to produce and publish writing, including in collaboration with peers" (CCSS ELA-Literacy.w.2.6).

Note: This collection of poems has multiple concrete poems from which primary students can gather ideas. Many shapes are simple.

1. Show students the cover of the book, asking students if they think the book may include serious poems or humorous ones. Have them explain by commenting on the illustration details and title.
2. Project page 25 so all students can see and read the poem.
   a. Lead students in open-ended questions, commenting about its shape and illustrations.
      i. Looking at the shape, what is the topic of the poem?
      ii. Do the illustrations imply that the topic brings joy to kids? Explain your stance.
      iii. Reading the title, what do you think the poet is going to be telling readers? Explain.
      iv. Do you think the title of the poem should be "Sprinkler" instead of "All wet"? Explain.
   b. Read the entire poem to the students and lead students in open-ended discussion.
      i. Were we correct when we decided that the topic brings joy to the kids? Explain.

    ii.   What do you notice about the words: *clean, crisp, cold*? What do we call it when writers use the same initial letter/sound in a number of words in a line?

    iii. Is there any other alliteration in the poem? If so, where?

    iv. What do you notice about the words *running, splashing, sliding* in the third line?

    v.   What does *bliss* mean? Does that reveal the mood of the poem?

    vi. Reread the poem and use expressions and gestures that fit the poem.

3. Pass out Figure 5.7, pair students, and give them five minutes to think of other types of concrete poems they could write.

4. Additional Mentor Texts

    a. Atwood, M., & Bigalk, K. (2011). *Connor and Clara build concrete poems*. Norwood House. Connor and Clara are enjoying teaching each other ways to build different types of concrete poems. This book has different shapes that are easy for students to replicate.

    b. Early Macken, J. (2015). *Read, recite, write concrete poems*. Crabtree Publishers. This book not only has examples of concrete poems but also gives teachers ideas on how to teach students to write concrete poems.

    c. Raczka, B. (2016). *Wet cement: A mix of concrete poems*. Roaring Brook Press. This is good mentor text for advanced students because the shapes are somewhat challenging; however, a couple of good poems for all primary students are on pages 5 ("Clock"), 13 ("Hanger"), and 41 ("Balloon"). These are easy shapes for the student to draw.

Mentor Text: "All Wet" in *Ode to a Commode: Concrete Poems.*

Author: Brian Cleary

Pair students to brainstorm ideas for possible concrete poem titles.

Have them keep the worksheet with their other IDEA papers so have ideas for future writing.

Concrete Poems

Topics	Shapes

GENRE: POETRY
FIGURE 5.7

6

Elementary Poetry

Introduction

The content of poems is as vast as the objects, experiences, emotions, and attitudes that surround us. By the time students are in the intermediate elementary grades, they should have been introduced to a wide array of poem topics. Thus, I chose Yolen's "One lone elk" from *Count me a rhyme: Animal poems by the numbers* (2006b). Not many students would consider writing a poem about an elk, but Yolen with the use of photographs and other creative features helps students understand that poems can be about any topic. The additional mentor texts include poem books about pirates, cities, and creatures' reflections.

There are many ways to organize a collection of poems. Teachers can encourage students to contribute a poem for a class collection that is organized around the topic of bugs, shapes, or colors found in the four seasons. Using the open-ended discussion questions in the mini-lesson will help students understand that poems can be organized in a wide array of ways.

Jack Prelutsky uses vivid word choices in his poems. The hilarious poem "The turkey shot out of the oven" in *Something big has been here* (1990) uses vivid verbs that may be unfamiliar to students; however, many of the verbs' meanings can be determined by the context of the poem. Two of the additional mentor poems are also by Prelutsky and the third is by Hopkins. Many school and community libraries have Prelutsky's and

DOI: 10.4324/9781003283478-6

Hopkin's poem books so these poems should be easy for teachers to find.

I hope all teachers will be able to locate "Foul shot" on the Internet or from the book. It is a topic with which many elementary students will be able to identify. This poem has a strong voice from a basketball audience as a player stands at the free-throw line to make a shot that will determine if the team wins or loses the game. There is much tension displayed in this short poem. The three additional poems also demonstrate strong voices as a baseball player steals his way around the diamond and as sailors are marooned on an island and then captured by pirates.

The featured mentor poem "The toy eater" in *Falling up* (Silverstein, 1996b) is an excellent poem to demonstrate how sentence fluency is used in poems. This poem features longer sentences through the use of series. The additional mentor texts feature the poets Hopkins and Prelutsky with another one by Silverstein.

The sixth trait, conventions, is found in Silverstein's "Mirror, mirror" in *Falling up* (1996c). This poem, written as a script, features the dialogue between two characters, the Mirror and the Queen. Scripts use a special format. It is best taught if teachers assign two students the parts of Queen and Mirror and then have them read the poem with appropriate expression. The additional mentor poems demonstrate how poets include quotation marks, question marks, and exclamation marks within direct quotations.

There are many ways to present poems so they have eye appeal. The featured poem is a concrete poem about an ice cream cone. The open-ended discussion will have students consider if there is a different way to present the same information. Teachers want elementary students to think creatively when they read and write poems. One of the additional mentor texts features acrostic poems that are not written with the name of the topic as the first letter of the lines; other creative ways are demonstrated. Another additional poem book features many types of poetic forms, including concrete and acrostic poems. The third text features concrete poems with shapes ranging from simple to difficult; there is a shape for all the varying abilities in the class.

Grade Level: Elementary
Trait: Content
Genre: Poetry
Mentor Text: *Count Me a Rhyme: Animal Poems by the Numbers*
Author: Jane Yolen (2006a)
Objective: "Produce clear and coherent writing in which the development and organization are appropriate to task, purpose, and audience" (CCSS.ELA-Literacy.W.5.4).

Procedure:

1. Read the title (*Count me a rhyme*) without showing the cover and lead students in an open-ended question.
   a. What do you think this book is about? Explain.
2. Show students the title page and have students predict the organization of the book.
3. Show and read the first poem to the class and lead them in an open-ended discussion.
   a. What do you view on these two pages?
   b. What do you think about the word choice?
   c. How many different ways is *one* displayed on the page?
   d. Was an elk a good animal to choose for the first poem? Explain.
4. Page through the book, having students comment on the photographs, the topic of the poems, the different ways the number are written, and the organization of the book.
5. Read the last poem "Many" and lead students in an open-ended discussion.
   a. Is this a good title?
   b. Is there a better title?
   c. Are there other words that you would include? Record their ideas on the board.

    d. What do you think about this poem?

    e. Are questions effective in the poem?

6. What other poem could you write for "100"?

    a. Pair students and have them complete Figure 6.1.

7. What is unique about the poems in this book that you have not seen in other collections of poem books?

8. Additional Mentor Poem Books

    a. Harrison, D. (2008c). *Pirates*. Wordsong. This book is a collection of poems that tell the story of pirates that attack a ship.

    b. Hopkins, L. B. (2009a). *City I love*. Abrams Books for Young Readers. This collection reflects unique characteristics of different cities around the world.

    c. Yolen, J. (2009). *A mirror to nature: Poems about reflection*. Wordsong. This mentor text is a collection of beautiful photographs in which creatures in nature are standing by water so readers can see its reflection in the water. Yolen writes poems that include ideas of the creature's reflecting on itself in a unique way. Students can see that poems can be about any topic.

Genre: Poetry

Mentor Text: *Count Me a Rhyme: Animal Poems by the Numbers*

Author: Jane Yolen

Photographs	Words for 100	Possible Lines in Poem

TRAIT: CONTENT
FIGURE 6.1

Grade Level: Elementary

Trait: Organization

Genre: Poetry

Mentor Text: *Bug off! Creepy, crawly poems*

Author: Jane Yolen (2012)

Objective: "Introduce a topic clearly, providing a general observation and focus, and group related information logically; include formatting, illustrations, and multimedia when useful to aiding comprehension"(CCSS.ELA-Literacy.W.5.2.a).

Procedure:

1. Without showing the cover or reading the title of the book, read the Table of Contents and ask students what they think the book is about.
2. Read the poem on p. 25: *Pop! Goes the tick.*
   a. Discuss what students learned about ticks (e.g. mostly mouth, suck blood, give people bacteria).
3. Discuss how poems can be sources of information.
4. Read the information shared on page 25 that is not part of the poem.
   a. What additional information did they learn?
   b. Discuss how Yolen gives readers information on how to remove a tick. Look up the cdc.gov website with them and instruct them on how to use the SEARCH box to find information about a tick.
5. Have students talk to their nearest classmate and have them discuss what other topic besides bugs they could use for a poem. Let them record in Figure 6.2.
   a. Would they first research the topic and then write a short passage, or would they first attempt to write a poem and then research the topic for more information? Explain.

6. Additional Mentor Texts
   a. Cleary, B. (2015e). *Ode to a commode: Concrete poems*. M. Millbrook Press. The poems in this book are all concrete poems. Students who enjoy writing this type of poem will get many ideas for writing concrete poems.
   b. Lewis, J. P. (Ed.). (2012). *Book of animal poetry*. National Geographic. This includes 169 pages of poems about animals. Pages 170–171 give students ideas of what type of poem (e.g. limerick, concrete, haiku, couplets) they can use to write about animals.
   c. Sidman, J. (2009). *Red sings from treetops: A year in colors*. Houghton Mifflin Books for Children. This book is written on the topics of seasons and colors. It also demonstrates how students can include different figures of speech.

Mentor Text: *Bug off! Creepy, crawly poems*

Author: Jane Yolen

Brainstormed ideas for possible content of a book of poems

Possible Topics	Types of Illustrations

TRAIT: CONTENT
FIGURE 6.2

Grade Level: Elementary
Trait: Word Choice
Genre: Poetry
Mentor Text: "The Turkey Shot Out of the Oven" in *Something Big Has Been Here*
Author: Jack Prelutsky (1990)
Objective: "Use concrete words and phrases and sensory details to convey experiences and events precisely" (CCSS Writing Standard for Literature 5.3.d.).

Procedure:

1. Read with expression and use gestures as you read the poem!
2. Discuss the following open-ended questions.
   a. Was it effective for Prelutsky to put the reason for the turkey shooting out of the oven at the very end of the poem? Explain.
   b. Would the poem be as humorous if Prelutsky started the poem with that line? Explain.
   c. What words do you think were excellent word choice to create humor?
   d. Do you know the meaning of the following words? Ricocheted, obscuring, blanketed, appliance, chagrin.
   e. Discuss the following phrases and how the verbs add to the humor of the poem and aid the readers as they visualize the action of the poem:
      i. "rocketed"
      ii. "ricocheted"
      iii. "obscuring"
      iv. "coated"
      v. "blanketed"

f. Using the table found in Figure 6.3, ask students to think of other words they could use that would create a vivid picture in the readers' minds.

g. Give students the opportunity to share their ideas.

h. Additional Mentor Poems

    i. Hopkins, L. (2009c). "Snow city" (third to last poem) in *City I love*. Harry N. Abrams, Inc. Hopkins uses vivid descriptions for the magic of falling snow in the city.

    ii. Prelutsky, J. (1984a). "I've got an incredible headache" (p. 46) in *The new kid on the block*. Greenwillow. This mentor poem has descriptive verbs and adjectives to describe a very bad headache.

    iii. Prelutsky, J. (1996). "I made something strange with my chemistry set" (pp. 58–59) in *A pizza the size of the sun*. Greenwillow Books. This mentor poem has many descriptive verbs to show readers the action of the narrator as he makes something with his chemistry set.

Genre: Poetry

Mentor Text: "The Turkey Shot Out of the Oven" in *Something Big Has Been Here*

Author: Jack Prelutsky

Words from Poem	Replacement	Replacement	Replacement
Rocketed			
Demolished			
Ricocheted			
Deafening boom			
Obscuring			
Coated			
Blanketed			
Smeared			
Chagrin			

TRAIT: WORD CHOICE
FIGURE 6.3

Grade Level: Elementary

Trait: Voice

Genre: Poetry

Mentor Text: "Foul Shot" in *Reflections on a gift of a water-melon pickle*

https://sites.google.com/site/middleschoolpoetryunit/3-integration-of-knowledge-and-ideas/1-analyze-how/foul-shot

OR

Dunning, S., Lueders, E., & Smith, H. (1967). *Reflections on a gift of a watermelon pickle . . . and other modern verse.*

Author/Illustrator: Edwin A. Hoey (1962)

Objective: "Use concrete words and phrases and sensory details to convey experiences and events precisely" (CCSS 5.3.d).

Procedure:

1. Using the website, project the poem so students can view how Hoey shows tension by how he writes the lines.
2. As you discuss the poem, have students take notes on Figure 6.4.
3. Read the entire poem with expression as if you are standing at the free-throw line; use body language to show the emotions and tension.
   a. Ask students if they ever experienced the pressure as displayed in the poem.
   b. Discuss the phrase "squeezed by silence." What does that mean? How does that add to the tension?
   c. Discuss the action of each line as the player stands on the free-throw line. How do the short lines followed by a comma add to the tension that the player is experiencing?

    d. Is "nudge" a vivid verb to use? Is there a better one? If so, what?

    e. Ask students to comment on the single-word lines as the player releases the ball.

    f. Discuss how Hoey's word choice adds to the suspense that is felt by everyone in the gym.

    g. Did Hoey spoil the tension by stating: "Right before ROAR-UP."

    If so, what other way the poem could end?

4. Additional Mentor Poems

    a. Francis, R. (1967). "The base stealer" (p. 112) in Dunning, S., Lueders, E., & Smith, H. (Eds.). (1967). *Reflections on a gift of a watermelon pickle . . . and other modern verse*. Lothrop, Lee & Shepard Co. This mentor poem demonstrates a strong voice of a baseball player stealing a base.

    b. Harrison, D. (2008b). "Marooned" (seventeenth poem) in David L. Harrison *Pirates*. Wordsong. This poem is a lament of a sailor as he is marooned on the shore. The last stanza has advice for all who break rules.

    c. Harrison, D. (2008a). "Captured" (twentieth poem) in David L. Harrison (Ed.), *Pirates*. Wordsong. This poem is a lament of a sailor who has been captured.

Trait: Voice

Genre: Poetry

Mentor Text: "Foul Shot" at

https://sites.google.com/site/middleschoolpoetryunit/3-integration-of-knowledge-and-ideas/1-analyze-how/foul-shot

OR

Dunning, S., Lueders, E., & Smith, H. (1967). *Reflections on a gift of a watermelon pickle . . . and other modern verse.*

Author/Illustrator: Edwin A. Hoey

1. Project the poem, using the following website., or from the book, if you have the book.

   https://sites.google.com/site/middleschoolpoetryunit/3-integration-of-knowledge-and-ideas/1-analyze-how/foul-shot

2. Pair students and ask them to write the words in the poem that vividly expresses tension. In the second column, have them record another word that could be used.

Word from Poem That Expresses the Player's Voice or Tension	*Possible Other Choice of Word*

GRADE LEVEL: ELEMENTARY
FIGURE 6.4

Grade Level: Elementary
Trait: Sentence Fluency
Genre: Poetry
Mentor Text: "The Toy Eater" in *Falling Up* (1996b, p. 77)
Author / Illustrator: Shel Silverstein
Objective: "Expand, combine, and reduce sentences for meaning, reader/listener interest, and style" (CCSS. ELA-Literacy.L.5.3.a).

Procedure:

1. Using the poem from the book, project the poem so all students can see it.
2. Read the poem with appropriate expression, observing the punctuation marks.
3. Discuss the sentence length by leading them in open-ended questions.
   a. How many lines is the first sentence?
   b. How many lines is the second sentence?
   c. What kind of clauses does Silverstein use in the second sentence?
   d. What type of sentence construction did Silverstein use to describe what the Terrible Toy-Eatin' Tookle did and ate?
   e. What type of sentence construction did Silverstein use at the end of the poem?
4. Read the poem as if each thought is a simple sentence (use a "period" stop)
   a. How different did it sound?
   b. Which way sounds best? Why?
   c. Invite a student to read it as written, observing punctuation.
   d. Did it sound different?

  e. Pair your students and ask them to add three or more lines to the beginning line of the poem found in Figure 6.5.

5. Additional Mentor Poems

  a. Hopkins, L. B. (2009b). "Sing a song of cities" (first poem) in Lee Bennett Hopkins (Ed.), *City I love*. Abrams Book of Young Readers. This short poem demonstrates the use of a series to create fluent writing.

  b. Prelutsky, J. (1984b). "Oh, teddy bear" (pp. 110–111) in Jack Prelutsky (Ed.), *The new kid on the block*. Greenwillow. Each of the three stanzas of the poem is one compound sentence. It is a good poem to demonstrate how compound sentences with the use of commas make for fluent writing.

  c. Silverstein, S. (1974c). "The unicorn" (pp. 76–77) in Shel Silverstein (Ed.), *Where the sidewalk ends*. HarperCollins. The poem has multiple examples of compound and complex sentences that make for fluent writing.

Genre: Poetry

Mentor Text: "The Toy Eater" in *Falling Up* (1996b, p. 77)

Author/Illustrator: Shel Silverstein

Parody of "The toy eater"

You said I don't have to clean my locker/desk?

_____

_____

TRAIT: SENTENCE FLUENCY
FIGURE 6.5

Grade Level: Elementary

Trait: Conventions

Genre: Poetry

Mentor Text: "Mirror, Mirror" in *Falling Up.*

Author/Illustrator: Shel Silverstein

Objective: "Use narrative techniques, such as dialogue, descriptions, and pacing, to develop experiences and events or show the responses of characters to situations" (CCSS. ELA-Literacy.W.5.3.b).

Procedure:

1. Using the book, project the poem so all students can see how it is written.
2. Invite a student to read the Queen's part and another to read the Mirror's part.
3. Lead students in an open-ended discussion with the following questions.
   a. On what nursery rhyme is this based?
   b. What do you think about the word choice that Silverstein used in the Queen's second verse?
   c. Will someone re-read it as if the Queen is answering her own question?
   d. What is the attitude of the Queen in the second verse?
   e. What is the Mirror's attitude in the second verse?
   f. What do the ellipses indicate in this verse? How do they redirect the speaker's train of thought?
   g. What do the dashes and parenthesis indicate in the last verse? Do they help the reader understand the panic that the Mirror was in?
4. Discuss if the script format is helpful in setting the mood and in understanding the poem. Have them explain their answers.

5. Bring attention to Silverstein's use of ellipsis and dashes.
6. Pair students and ask them what other familiar nursery rhyme they could rewrite, using the format of a script.
7. After five minutes, ask students to share.
   a. Hand out the table in Figure 6.6 so they can record their classmates' ideas and come back to this page when they are looking for an idea for a poem.
8. Additional Mentor Poems
   a. Hopkins, L. B. (2009d). "Taxi!" (sixth poem) in *City I love*. Abrams Books for Young readers. This poem demonstrates how to include direct quotations in a poem.
   b. Silverstein, S. (1986a). "Forgetful Paul Revere" (p. 122) in Shel Silverstein (Ed.), *Falling up*. HarperCollins. This poem demonstrates how questions can be written in a poem.
   c. Silverstein, S. (1974d). "What's in the sack?" (p. 111) in Shel Silverstein (Ed.), *Where the sidewalk ends*. HarperCollins. This demonstrates how students can incorporate both questions and direct quotations in a poem. It shows the correct punctuation marks to use for questions and direct quotes.

Trait: Conventions

Genre: Poetry

Mentor Text: "Mirror, Mirror" in *Falling Up* (1996c).

Author/Illustrator: Shel Silverstein

http://poemsbyshelsilverstein.blogspot.com/2009/01/poem-by-shel-silverstein-pg-88.html

Fairy Tale	Possible Characters for Script

GRADE LEVEL: ELEMENTARY
FIGURE 6.6

Grade Level: Elementary

Trait: Presentation

Genre: Poetry

Mentor Text: "Cool, Sweet . . . But Enough About Me" in *Ode to a Commode: Concrete Poems* (2015c).

Author: Brian Cleary

Objective: "Analyze how visual and multimedia elements contribute to the meaning, tone, or beauty of a text (e.g. graphic novel, multimedia presentation of fiction, folktale, myths, poems" (CCSS.ELA-Literacy.L.5.7).

Note to teachers: If this book of concrete poems is not in your school or community library, it is a good one to get for your classroom library. All the concrete poems are shapes students can easily use as mentors.

Procedure:

1. Show students the cover of the book, and ask them if they think the book may include serious poems or humorous ones. Have them explain by commenting on the illustration details and title.
2. Project page 27 so all students can see and read the poem.
   a. Lead students in open-ended questions, commenting about shapes and illustrations.
      i. Looking at the shape, what is the topic of the poem?
      ii. Do you think the ice cream will fall off the cone? Explain.
      iii. Reading the title, what do you think the poet is going to be telling readers in this poem? Explain.
      iv. Do the illustrations give readers more clues about the information Cleary shares? Explain.
3. Invite a student to read the poem.

    a. Lead students in an open-ended discussion about the word choice.

        i. Are all of these ice cream flavors possible? If not, which ones are too strange to be possible?

        ii. Do the flavors add to the tone of the poem? Explain.

        iii. Would you save vanilla as the last possible flavor? Explain.

        iv. Why do you suppose Cleary added in parenthesis: "It's rather close to lunch" after the peanut butter swirl?

        v. What other flavor would you add?

        vi. Would it be better if Cleary wrote the poem from the bottom to top? Explain.

        vii. What other way could you illustrate this poem? (Let students come to the board to show the shape they would choose.)

4. Pass out Figure 6.7, pair students, and ask them to think of other concrete poem titles/shapes.

5. If time permits, invite students to come to the board to draw their shape.

6. Additional Mentor Texts

    a. Harley, A. (2009). *African acrostic: A word in edgeways*. Candlewick Press. Each poem is written as an acrostic poem with new twists. Not every poem gives the animal's name going down; some poems express unique traits of the African animal with the acrostic being formed with the first line, then second line, then third line, and so on. The photographs are close-ups of the animal in its natural habitat.

    b. Raczka, B. (2016). *Wet cement: A mix of concrete poems*. Roaring Brook Press. All the poems in this book are concrete poems with shapes easy for students to replicate and to write concrete poems.

    c. Janeczko, P. (2005). *A kick in the head: An everyday guide to poetic forms*. Candlewick Press. This mentor text has many types of poetic forms, including concrete and acrostic poems.

Mentor Text: "Cool, Sweet . . . But Enough About Me" in *Ode to a Commode: Concrete Poems.*

Author/Illustrator: Brian Cleary

Other Possible Titles and Shapes for Concrete Poems

Title	Shape

FIGURE 6.7

Final Takeaways

You have been introduced to a small sliver of possible mentor texts you can use to develop your students' writing skills. They need ample time to practice writing fiction, informational texts, and poems. It was a difficult task for me to select one featured title for each lesson. If you could view my computer files you would see that I have extensive files for each of the six chapters. Hopefully, as you read to students, encounter new texts, and observe what your students are reading, you will keep adding new mini lessons to these. I encourage you to use these mini lessons during Guided Writing and Writers Workshop. I would enjoy visiting with you to see what texts you substitute for the ones I featured. I encourage you to substitute titles based on your students' interests and writing skills.

As with any "suggested" lesson plans, these mini-lessons should be modified to meet the needs of your students. If you teach fifth grade, you may find that some of the mini-lessons in the primary chapters are more appropriate for a small group of your reluctant writers. If you teach primary grades, you may find that your advanced writers would benefit from some of the elementary chapters. Hopefully you use small groups to teach writing, just like you use small groups to teach reading and math. Highly qualified teachers understand that no two students learn and develop literacy skills in the same manner.

Finally, I encourage you to use open-ended questions to guide your students to examine and discover what authors do when they write. I also encourage you to listen to your students' responses as you teach these mini lessons; their responses may lead you down a path different from the written lesson, and that is good! Follow their lead! Students often teach us a thing or two as we work with them.

References

Alexander, L. (2000). *How the cat swallowed thunder*. Puffin Books.

Allgor, M. (2013). *Endangered desert animals*. PowerKids Press.

American Museum of Natural History. (2014). *ABC insects*. American Museum of Natural History.

Atwood, M., & Bigalk, K. (2011). *Connor and Clara build concrete poems*. Norwood House.

Barrett, J. (1982). *Cloudy with a chance of meatballs*. Atheneum Books for Young Readers.

Bassier, E. (2020). *Dolphins!* Cody Koala/Pop!

Bennett, J. (1987). *Noisy poems*. Oxford Press.

Boelts, M. (2007). *Those shoes*. Candlewick Press.

Bowman, C. (2015). *North American animals: Bald eagles*. Bellwether Media.

Brett, J. (1989). *The mitten*. G. P. Putnam's Sons.

Brett, J. (1997). *The hat*. G. P. Putnam's Sons.

Brett, J. (2004). *The umbrella*. G. P. Putnam's Sons.

Brosgol, V. (2021). *Memory jars*. Roaring Brooks Press.

Campoy, E. I., & Howell, T. (2016). *Maybe something beautiful: How art transformed a neighborhood*. Houghton Mifflin Harcourt.

Chad, J. (2013). *Leo Geo and the cosmic crisis*. Roaring Brook Press.

Chute, M. Our tree. (1957). In B. Schenk de Regniers, M. Michaels White, & J. Carr (Eds.), *Sing a song of popcorn* (p. 27). Scholastic.

Cleary, B. (2015a). All wet. In *Ode to a commode: Concrete poems* (p. 25). Millbrook Press.

Cleary, B. (2015b). Brrrr. In *Ode to a commode: Concrete poems* (p. 18). Millbrook Press.

Cleary, B. (2015c). Cool, sweet . . . but enough about me. In *Ode to a commode: Concrete poems* (p. 27). Millbrook Press.

Cleary, B. (2015d). What about me? In *Ode to a commode: Concrete poems* (p. 9). Millbrook Press.

Cleary, B. (2015e). *Ode to a commode: Concrete poems*. Millbrook Press.

Clements, A. (2007). *Dogku*. Simon & Schuster Books for Young Readers.

Cooling, W. (2010). *All the wild wonders: Poems of our earth*. Francis Lincoln Children's Books.

Cousteau, P., & Hopkinson, D. (2016). *Follow the moon home: A tale of one idea, twenty kids, and a hundred sea turtles*. Chronicle Books.

Craft, J. (2019). *New kid*. HarperCollins Publishing.

Creech, S. (1994). *Walk two moon*. HarperCollins Publishing.

Cummings, T. (2018). *Can I be your dog?* Random House.

Curtis, C. P. (1999). *Bud, not buddy*. Delacorte Press.

Daywait, D. (2013). *The day the crayons quit*. Philomel.

De Medeiros, J. (2022). *Dolphins*. AV2 Books.

dePaola, T. (1975). *The cloud book*. Holiday House.

dePaola, T. (1977). *The quick sand book*. Holiday House.

dePaola, T. (1978). *The popcorn book*. Holiday House.

dePaola, T. (1979). *The kids' cat book*. Holiday House.

Doyon, S. C. (2020). *Magnificent homespun brown: A celebration* (K. Juanita, Illus.). Tilbury House Publishers.

Dunning, S., Lueders, E., & Smith, H. (Eds.). (1967). *Reflections on a gift of a watermelon pickle . . . and other modern verse*. Lothrop, Lee & Shepard Co.

Early Macken, J. (2015). *Read, recite, write concrete poems*. Crabtree Publishers.

Erickson, J. R. (1983). *The original adventure of Hank the cowdog*. Maverick.

Farmer, J. (1999). *Bananas*. Bt. Bound.

Fleming, D. (1998). *In the small, small pond*. Henry Holt.

Floca, B. (2009). *Moonshot*. A Richard Jackson Book, Atheneum Books for Young Readers.

Floca, B. (2013). *The locomotive*. A Richard Jackson Book, Atheneum Books for Young Readers. Corr.

Flood, J. (2018). *Science comics: Sharks: Nature's perfect hunter*. First Second.

Flor Ada, A. (1994). Dear baby bear. In *Dear Peter Rabbit*. Atheneum Books for Young Children.

Francis, R. (1967). The base stealer. In S. Dunning, E. Lueders, & H. Smith (Eds.), *Reflections on a gift of a watermelon pickle . . . and other modern verse* (p. 112). Lothrop, Lee & Shepard Co.

George, M. (2007). *Bats*. The Child's World.

Gerstein, M. (2003). *The man who walked between the towers*. Roaring Brook Press.

Harley, A. (2009). *African acrostics: A word in edgeways*. Candlewick Press.

Harrison, D. (2008a). Captured. In *Pirates* (p. 2 to last poem). Wordsong.

Harrison, D. (2008b). Marooned. In *Pirates* (p. 5 to last poem). Wordsong.

Harrison, D. (2008c). *Pirates*. Wordsong.

Henkes, K. (1995). *Julius, the baby of the world*. Greenwillow.

Henkes, K. (1996). *Lilly's purple plastic purse*. Greenwillow.

Henkes, K. (2008). *Chrysanthemum*. Greenwillow.

Herrington, L. M. (2015). *Turtles and tortoises*. Children's Press.

Hircsh, A. (2017). *Science comics: Dogs from predator to protector*. First Second.

Hoey, E. A. (1962). Foul shot. In S. Dunning, E. Lueders, & H. Smith (Eds.), *Reflections on a gift of a watermelon pickle . . . and other modern verse* (pp. 112–113). Lothrop, Lee & Shepard Co.

Hopkins, L. B. (2009a). *City I love*. Abrams Books for Young Readers.

Hopkins, L. B. (2009b). Sing a song of cities. In *City I love* (p. 1 poem). Abrams Books for Young Readers.

Hopkins, L. B. (2009c). Snow city. In *City I love* (p. 3 to last page). Abrams Books for Young Readers.

Hopkins, L. B. (2009d). Taxi! In *City I love* (6th poem). Abrams Books for Young Readers.

Hopkins, L. B. (2018). *A bunch of punctuation*. Wordsong.

Jackson, E. (2010). *A home for Dixie: The true story of a rescued puppy*. Turtleback Books.

Janeczko, P. (2005). *A kick in the head*. Candlewick Press.

Kennedy, X. J. (1975). The whales off wales. In *Book of animal poetry* (p. 28). National Geographic.

Knisley, L. (2020). *Stepping stones*. RH Graphics.

Kras, S. L. (2010). *Koalas*. Capstone Press.

Latchana Kenney, K. (2019). *Life cycle of a butterfly*. Pogo Books.

Lewis, J. P. (Ed.). (2012). *Book of animal poetry*. National Geographic.

Llewellyn, C. (2005). *Rainforest animals*. Sea-To-Sea.

Lockwood, S. (2006). *Sea turtles*. The Child's World.

Mafi, T. (2016). *Furthermore*. Dutton Children's Books.

Mann, J. K. (2020). *The camping trip*. Candlewick Press.

Markert, J. (2007a). *Cheetahs*. The Child's World.

Markert, J. (2007b). *Elephants*. The Child's World.

Marsh, L. (2015). *Alligators and crocodiles*. National Geographic Kids.

McCarthy, M. (2010). *Pop! The invention of bubble gum*. A Paula Wiseman Book, Simon & Schuster Books for Young Readers.

Mills, A. (2018). *The everything book of cats and kittens*. DK Penguin Random House.

Moore, L. (1988). Until I saw the sea. In B. Schenk de Regniers, M. Michaels White, & J. Carr (Eds.), *Sing a song of popcorn* (p. 115). Scholastic.

Murray, P. (2007). *Frogs*. The Child's World.

National Geographic (2012). *Book of animal poetry*. National Geographic.

Newman, P. (2017). *Sea otter heroes: The predators that saved an ecosystem*. Milbrook Press.

Numeroff, L. J. (1985). *If you give a mouse a cookie*. HarperCollins.

Numeroff, L. J., & Evans, N. (2008). *The jellybeans and the big dance*. Scholastic.

O'Neill, M. (1961). What is yellow? In *Hailstones and halibut bones* (second to last poem in book). Doubleday.

Osborne, W., & Pope Osborne, M. (2003). *Twisters and other terrible storms*. Random House.

Peak, R. (2000). *A year down yonder*. Puffin.

Pilkey, D. (2017). *Dog man unleashed*. Graphix, Scholastic.

Polacco, P. (2005). *Emma Kate*. Philomel Books.

Pope Osborne, M., & Pope Boyce, N. (2003). *Dolphins and sharks*. A Stepping Stone Book, Random House.

Pope Osborne, M., & Pope Boyce, N. (2008). *Sea monsters*. Random House.

Portis, A. (2020). *A new green day*. Neal Portis Books.

Prelutsky, J. (1984a). I've got an incredible headache. In *The new kid on the block* (p. 46). Greenwillow.

Prelutsky, J. (1984b). Oh, teddy bear. In *The new kid on the block* (pp. 110–111). Greenwillow.

Prelutsky, J. (1988). The spaghetti nut. In B. Schenk de Regniers, M. Michaels White, & J. Carr (Eds.), *Sing a song of popcorn* (p. 109). Scholastic.

Prelutsky, J. (1990). The turkey shot out of the oven. In *Something big has been here* (pp. 18–19). Greenwillow.

Prelutsky, J. (1996). I made something strange with my chemistry set. In *A pizza the size of the sun* (pp. 58–59). Greenwillow.

Raczka, B. (2016). *Wet cement: A mix of concrete poems*. Roaring Brook Press.

Reeve, J. (1988). The old wife and the ghost. In B. Schenk de Regniers, M. Michaels White, & J. Carr (Eds.), *Sing a song of popcorn* (pp. 40–42). Scholastic.

Rey, M., & Rey, H. A. (2004). *A treasury of Curious George*. Houghton Mifflin Company.

Reynolds, A. (2014). *Pirates vs. cowboys*. Alfred A. Knopf.

Reynolds, P. H. (2003). *The dot*. Candlewick Press, AV2 Books.

Reynolds, P. H. (2018). *The word collector*. Orchard Books.

Richardson, C., & Richardson, D. (2021). *Family reunion* (A. Corrin, Illus.). Barefoot Books.

Rosenstock, B. (2021). *Moments with Monet* (M. Grandpre, Illus.). Alfred A. Knope.

Salley, C. (2004). *Why Epossumondas has no hair on his tail*. Harcourt, Inc.

Sandburg, C. (1988). We must be polite. In B. Schenk de Regniers, M. Michaels White, & J. Carr (Eds.), *Sing a song of popcorn* (p. 96). Scholastic.

Schenk de Regniers, B., Michaels White, M., & Carr, J. (Eds.). (1988). *Sing a song of popcorn*. Scholastic.

Schnur, S. (2002). *Winter: An alphabet acrostic*. Clarion Books.

Shannon, D. (2012). *Jangles: A big fish story*. The Blue Sky Press, Scholastic.

Sidman, J. (2009). *Red sings from treetops: A year in colors*. Houghton Mifflin Books for Children.

Siemens, J. (2022a). *Humpback whales*. AV2 Books.

Siemens, J. (2022b). *Sea turtles*. AV2 Books.

Silverstein, S. (1974a). Ickle me, pickle me, tickle me too. In *Where the sidewalk ends* (pp. 16–17). HarperCollins Publishers.

Silverstein, S. (1974b). Snowman. In *Where the sidewalk ends* (p. 65). HarperCollins Publishers.

Silverstein, S. (1974c). The unicorn. In *Where the sidewalk ends* (pp. 76–77). HarperCollins Publishers.

Silverstein, S. (1974d). What's in the sack? In *Where the sidewalk ends* (p. 111). HarperCollins.

Silverstein, S. (1996a). Forgetful Paul Revere. In *Falling up* (p. 122). HarperCollins.

Silverstein, S. (1996b). The toy eater. In *Falling up* (p. 77). HarperCollins.

Silverstein, S. (1996c). Mirror, mirror. In *Falling up* (p. 88). HarperCollins.

Simon, S. (2015). *Frogs*. HarperCollins Publishers.

Stansfield, L. (2019). *Poems out loud: First poems to read and perform*. Ladybird.

Stevens, J., & Stevens Crummel, S. (1999). *Cook-a-doodle-doo!* Harcourt Brace & Company.

Sweet, M. (2011). *Balloons over Broadway: The story of the puppeteer of Macy's Parade*. A Junior Library Guild Selection.

Thomson, S. (2006). *Amazing dolphins!* HarperCollins Publishers.

Wardlaw, L. (2015). *Won ton and chopstick: A cat and dog tale told in haiku* (E. Yelchin, Illus.). Henry Holt & Company.

Wicks, M. (2016). *Science comics: Coral reefs: Cities of the ocean*. First Second.

Willems, M. (2004). *The pigeon finds a hot dog!* Hyperion Books for Children.

Willems, M. (2019). *Because*. Hyperion Books for Children.

Wood, A. (1984). *The napping house*. Harcourt Brace Jovanovich Publishers.

Wood, A. (2000). *Jubal's wish*. The Blue Sky Press.

Yolen, J. (1992). *Encounter*. Voyager Books.

Yolen, J. (2006a). *Count me a rhyme: Animal poems by the numbers*. Wordsong, Boyds Mills Press.

Yolen, J. (2006b). One lone elk. In *Count me a rhyme: Animal poems by the numbers* (pp. 10–11). Wordsong, Boyds Mills Press.

Yolen, J. (2009). *A mirror to nature: Poems about reflection* (J. Stemple, Illus.). Wordsong, Boyds Mills Press.

Yolen, J. (2012). *Bug off! Creepy, crawly poems* (J. Stemple, Illus.). Word Song.

Zakroff, C. (2021). *Science comics: Whales: Diving into the unknown*. First Second.